Harry V. Vogt

By Force of Impulse

A Drama in Five Acts

Harry V. Vogt

By Force of Impulse
A Drama in Five Acts

ISBN/EAN: 9783337779788

Printed in Europe, USA, Canada, Australia, Japan

Cover: Foto ©Thomas Meinert / pixelio.de

More available books at **www.hansebooks.com**

FORCE OF IMPULSE.

A DRAMA IN FIVE ACTS.

BY
HARRY V. VOGT.

PRICE, 15 CENTS.

NEW YORK:
HAROLD ROORBACH, PUBLISHER,
9 MURRAY STREET.

BY FORCE OF IMPULSE.

CAST OF CHARACTERS.

MORRIS MAITLAND, A Stern Puritan, with unbending will, whose word is law.

REGINALD MAITLAND, - His Son; one of Nature's noblemen.

HENRY LOWVILLE, True as Steel; a little soured against the female sex, and a hater of "fashionable society."

RALPH MURDELL, - A polished, smooth tongued scoundrel.

COLONEL MORRELL, A True Soldier, with a keen sense of duty.

GEO. WASHINGTON DOLLERCLUTCH, An Eccentric Lawyer of the "Old School," who possesses a large, sympathetic heart.

SAMMY DEWDROP, The Son of a Millionaire; fresh from college, full of romantic nonsense.

ADOLPHUS SOFTHEAD, His Chum, whose mental faculties have not kept pace with his physical.

CORIOLANUS WELLINGTON, Who never smiles, and who thinks he was born to fill a higher station in life than that of menial.

ADRIENNE LOWVILLE, A Proud, Impulsive Beauty, who loves not wisely but too well.

HILDA WALLACE, Her Maid, whose birth is obscure. An innocent victim of misplaced love.

ANASTASIA MAITLAND, A Gushing Maiden of Forty-five Summers; very susceptible.

GUESTS, SOLDIERS, ETC., ETC.

SYNOPSIS.

ACT I. LOVE VERSUS IMPULSE.

ACT II. THE SEPARATION.

ACT III. DUTY VERSUS IMPULSE.

ACT IV. THE RECONCILIATION AND SEQUEL.

ACT V. DIVINE IMPULSE.

COSTUMES.

MORRIS MAITLAND.—Act II.—Plain dark suit, white cravat, long haired gray wig, quarter bald, close shaven face ; change coat for long wrapper in 3d Scene. Acts IV. and V.—Plain gray business suit, light slouch hat.

REGINALD MAITLAND.—Act I.—Black dress suit, black slouch hat. Act II.—Dark traveling suit. Acts III., IV. and V.—Uniform of a Private, U.S.A. Cloak to throw over uniform in 4th Act.

HENRY LOWVILLE.—Act I.—Rich hunting suit, gun, game bag, etc. Act II.—Uniform of a Recruiting Officer, U. S. A. Acts III. and V.—Uniform of a Captain, U. S. A.

RALPH MURDELL.—Act I.—Black dress suit, silk hat. Act II.—Genteel sack suit, derby hat. Acts III., IV. and V.—Uniform of a Major, U. S. A.

COLONEL MORRELL.—Uniform of a Colonel, U. S. A.

GEO. WASHINGTON DOLLERCLUTCH.—Acts I. and II.—Dark pants, dark cutaway coat, white vest, high collar and cravat, white silk hat, nose glasses, black crop wig, bald, close shaven face. Acts III., IV. and V.—Uniform of a Private, U. S. A. A cloak to throw over uniform in 4th Act.

SAMMY DEWDROP.—Act I.—Dark foppish suit, showy jewelry, stand-up collar and flashy necktie, cane, glasses, silk hat with narrow brim, red crop wig, close shaven face. Act II.—White linen suit, small brimmed straw hat with white band.

ADOLPHUS SOFTHEAD.—Act I.—Dark frock suit, small derby hat, very large stud in shirt front, heavy watch chain, large bouquet in button-hole, blonde crop wig, close shaven face. Act II.—Light sack suit, straw hat with blue band. Acts III. and V.—Uniform of a Private, U. S. A. Change coat and cap in 3d Act for a Rebel's.

CORIOLANUS WELLINGTON.—Act I.—Very seedy suit, à la shabby genteel, long haired black wig. Change in last scene to tight-fitting black suit, ruffled collar and cravat, white shoe guards, black square-crowned hat. Act II.—Same as second change in 1st Act, but change necktie during Act to a ridiculously large red necktie. Acts III. and V.—Uniform of a Private, U. S. A.

ADRIENNE LOWVILLE.—Act I.—Rich evening dress. Act II.—Handsome traveling dress. Acts IV. and V.—Plain white morning dress.

HILDA WALLACE.—Act I.—Very plain black cloth dress, no jewelry or ornaments, derby hat ; change in last scene to white apron and frilled cap. Act II.—Same as 1st, and change as before in last scene. Act IV.—Same as before, with slight changes. Act V.—Plain silk dress.

ANASTASIA MAITLAND.—Acts I. and II.—Old-fashioned black silk dress, large bonnet, large parasol and fan, wig with curls. Change bonnet in 2d Act for a frilled cap. Acts IV. and V.—Same as before with some changes.

PROPERTIES.

ACT I.—SCENE 1.—Writing materials, books, etc., on table. Lawyer's bag. papers, memorandums, etc., for Dollerclutch. Newspaper with written paragraph, also sealed letter, writing materials, etc., on desk. Baby dress and money for Hilda Wallace. Lunch for Coriolanus to bring on. SCENE 2.—Sign on tree. Segar-case and match-box for Reginald. SCENE 3.—Small valise with smelling-bottle in it for Coriolanus. Matches for Sammy Dewdrop. Memorandum tablet and pencil for Dollerclutch. Card-case for Ralph.

ACT II.—SCENE 1.—Bell on table. Knitting for Anastasia. Bundle and wraps for Hilda. SCENE 2.—Roll of draft, pencil and pistol for Henry. SCENE 3.—Memorandum tablet, pencil and baby dress for Dollerclutch. Letter for Anastasia. Pistol and roll of draft for Henry. Basket with broken glass off L. 2 E.

ACT III.—Card photograph for Reginald. Rebel hat and coat and whiskers and pieces of rope in L. 3 E. for Adolphus. Switch in L. 3 E. for Coriolanus. Pistol and baby dress for Dollerclutch. Large wallet containing two special papers, etc.; also, six letters for Ralph to bring on. Cloak in tent L. 4 E. for Dollerclutch, and one in tent L. 5 E. for Reginald.

ACT IV.—SCENE 1.—Pen, ink and paper on table. Knitting and letter for Anastasia. SCENE 2.—Cloak and two special papers and baby dress for Dollerclutch. SCENE 3.—Candles on table. Letter for Adrienne. Ring for Dollerclutch.

ACT V.—Map on table for officers. Bundle containing letter and envelope, with blackened paper and bullet in it, for Coriolanus to bring on. Seal ring and Ralph Murdell's left shoulder strap for Dollerclutch. Revolver at prompt R. 2 E. Two handkerchiefs for Adolphus. One handkerchief for Ralph.

SCENERY.

ACT I.

SCENE 1.—Dollerclutch's Office in 4th Grooves.

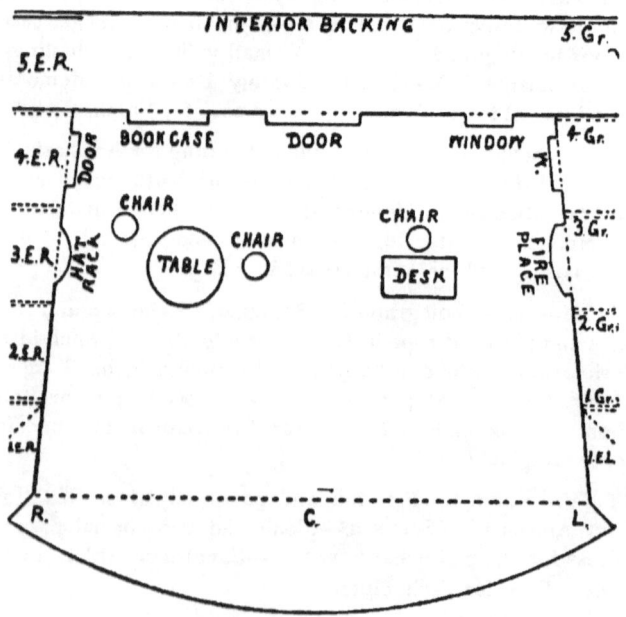

C. door in flat. Door, R. 4 E. Fireplace, L. 3 E. Window, L. F. and L. 4 E. Book-case against R. F. Hat-rack, R. 3 E. Desk and chair, L. C. Table and chairs, R. C.

SCENE 2.—A Wood-pass in 2d Grooves. Sign on tree, R. F.—"Beware! Do not disturb the Deer. Wm. Lowville."

6   *By Force of Impulse.*

SCENE 3.—(Entire Stage.)—Grounds adjoining Wm. Lowville's Mansion. Illuminated by colored lamps. Flat in 5th Grooves representing a terrace. The wings represent trees.

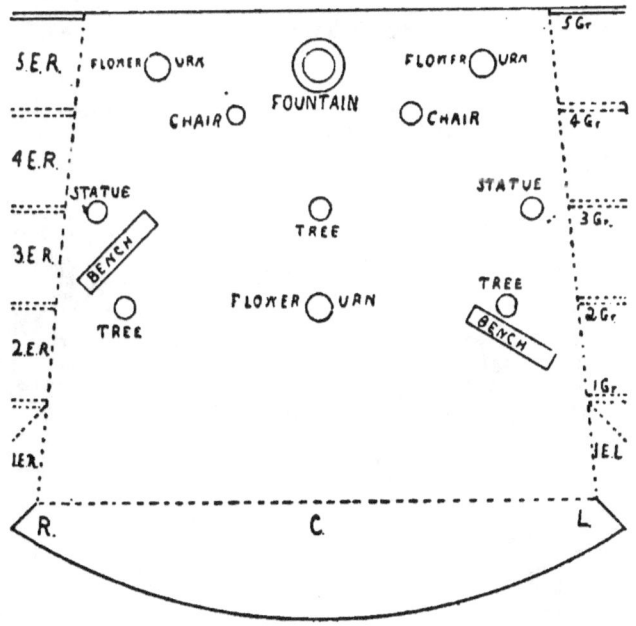

Fountain, statuary, flower urns, iron chairs, trees, etc. Rustic benches, R. 3 E. and L. 2 E.

ACT II.

Scene 1.—Sitting Room in the Maitland Cottage in 4 G. Plainly but substantially furnished. Scene backed by wood-scene in 5 G. Time, evening. Moonlight effect back of 4 G.

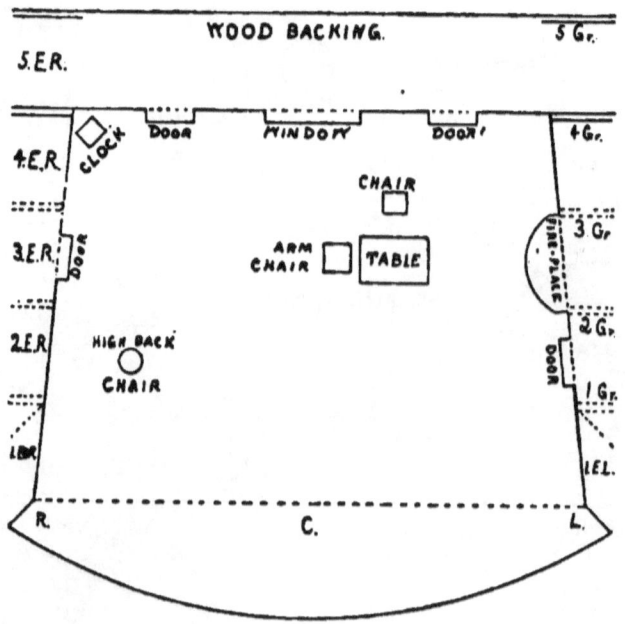

Large open window, C. of F. Glass doors, R. and L. F. Doors, L. 2 E. and R. 3 E. Fireplace, L. 3 E. Table and chairs, L. C. High-back chair, R. C. Old-fashioned clock, R. 4 E.

Scene 2.—Street Scene in 1 G.

Scene 3.—(Entire Stage.)—Outside of Maitland Cottage. Backed by wood-scene in 5 G. Plain cottage, with ivy and roses, on left. Time, morning.

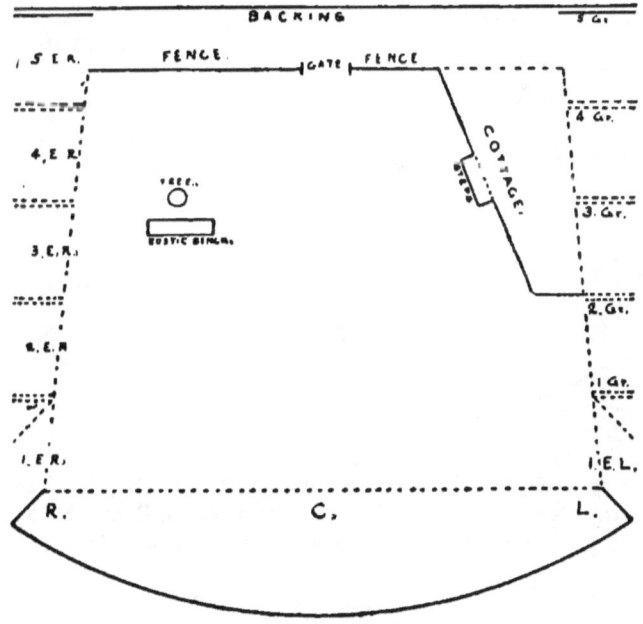

Picket fence, with gate in C., in the background. Rustic bench against tree, R. C.

ACT III.

Camp Scene.—(Entire Stage.)—Scene representing a rocky ravine.

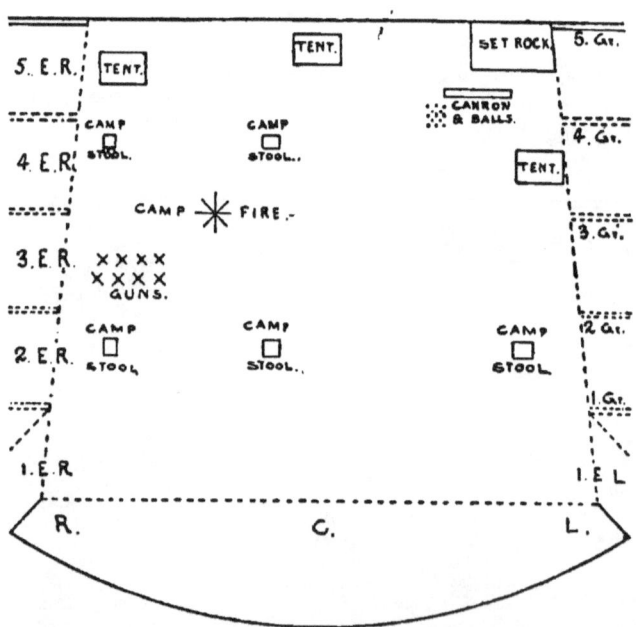

High set rock, L. 5 E. Cannon and cannon balls, L. 5 E. Tent, C., near flat. Tent, R. 5 E. and L. 4 E. Camp stools, R. C. 4 E., R. 4 E., R. 2 E., R. C. 2 E., L. 2 E. Camp-fire, R. C. 4 E. Stack of guns, R. 3 E.

ACT IV.

Scene 1.—(Same as 1st Scene, 2d Act, with addition of child's crib, L. 4 E.) Time, morning. Sunlight effect back of 4 G.

Scene 2.—Wood-pass in 1 G. Time, night.

Scene 3.—(Same as 1st Scene.) Time, night. Moonlight effect back of 4 G.

ACT V.

Camp Scene.—(Same as Act 3d, with addition of table and three camp stools R. 2 E.)

STAGE DIRECTIONS.

The player is supposed to be facing the audience. C., centre. R., right. L., left. R.C., right of centre. L.C., left of centre. D., door. R.D., right door. L.D., left door. C.D., centre door. F.D., door in flat. R.F.D., door in right flat. L.F.D., door in left flat. 1 E., first entrance. 2 E., second entrance. U.E., upper entrance. 1 G., first groove. 2 G., second groove. .

R.   R.C.   C.   L.C.   L.

NOTE.

The character of Coriolanus Wellington, to carry out successfully the idea of the author, should be played with an extreme degree of solemnity, so as to appear ludicrous. His action should be of the lofty and dignified order, but greatly overdrawn, and he should be decidedly mechanical in his movements and gestures.

BY FORCE OF IMPULSE.

ACT I.

Scene 1: DOLLERCLUTCH'S OFFICE.

Enter DOLLERCLUTCH, *D. R. 4 E.*, *with lawyer's bag. He empties his pockets of papers, etc., on desk, L. 3 E., while speaking.*

Dol. Now if that isn't confoundedly provoking, I'd just like to know what is. There I've been on a ninety-mile journey; and what did I gain? Nothing, absolutely nothing, and just to think of throwing away so much money for railroad travel, only to have the satisfaction of knowing that you have added to the pile of monopoly and have nothing in return. Confound these railroad companies anyhow! Honest people subscribe to the stock and build them; then come along these "stock jobbing sharks," who corner the stocks and put the road in their vest-pockets. And they call that business; but it's only another name for d—n robbery. But where is that confounded Coriolanus? [*Calls.*] Coriolanus! Coriolanus! Just like the rascal. Whenever you want him, nowhere to be found. When he is about, what good is he with his stuck up manners and airs? Thinks himself born to fill a higher sphere in life. But the only thing he's good for is to stand him in the entry and use him for a hat rack. Confound him anyhow! [*Calls.*] Coriolanus! [*Listens.*] Where the deuce can he be? To gratify him I answered an advertisement for a position, which, he says, would be more suitable for his intellectual and genteel qualities—and, if it is only successful I shall be well rid of the rascal. [*Picks up letter.*] Hello! just the thing, by jingo! [*Reads.*] "Terms satisfactory. If convenient come at once. The position is man-servant; but, as I am away at business during the day, I want a reliable and intelligent person to supervise the work about the premises, and be a protector to the females." That will just please him, and it will just please me to get rid of him. [CORIOLANUS *puts his head in C. door.*]

Cor. Was I mistaken, or did the sound of your voice penetrate the cavity of my ear?

Dol. Did I call? Well, if that ain't cool! Call? Of course I did!—and why the deuce didn't you come immediately?

CORIOLANUS **Enters.**

Cor. Because, my dear sir, I was otherwise engaged, and I felt assured that you would indulge me to that extent and postpone your desires to my especial accommodation. Thank you! [*With a wave of the hand.*]

Dol. Oh! and how in thunder were you engaged?

Cor. [*Loftily.*] I was paring my finger nails.

Dol. Oh! Oh! [*Falls in chair at desk.*] This is too much. To return travel-wearied and hungry, and be made to wait by such a jackass. And I must be at court at ten, and [*pulls out watch*] it's nine now. [*Starts up in a rage.*] I'll not stand it, sir! I'll throw you out of the window!

Cor. [*R. C.*] Indeed! Then I should be at a loss to wonder what could be the matter with the door. Stay your temper, sir! It is decidedly unbecoming a man of your years. Preserve a calm dignity such as I furnish a striking example of.

Dol. [*Disgusted.*] There, sir! [*Hands him letter.*] This is the gratitude I receive for what I have done for you. Read it, and I hope you will have as much joy of it as I have in getting rid of you.

Cor. Thank you! Thanks! You have performed your duty well. Some day I will return the kindness; I shall engage you as my lawyer.

Dol. Get out, or I shall be tempted to do you an injury. Get your things ready to leave to-night, sir! I'll not put up with your nonsense and impudence another day. Now go, sir! and order a lunch for me at the restaurant, to be sent here—and mind you see that I am not disturbed until court time. I've got more than I can do to prepare my cases for this morning's court. I may forget the flight of time, in which case you will please come in and remind me of court time.

Cor. Your wishes shall be obeyed. I fly to execute your orders. [**Exit** *D. R. 4 E.*]

Dol. [*At desk L. 3 E.*] George Washington, you're a fool —your magnanimous nature has suffered you to be imposed upon—you're a—[CORIOLANUS *puts his head in D. R. 4 E.*]

Cor. I beg your pardon, sir! [*He* **Enters.**] In the excitement of the moment I neglected to inform you that a lady called to see you. I informed her that you were out of town. She was much distressed at the information. She waited for you until eight o'clock, when she left in a state of great mental excitement. She's been waiting since six o'clock this morning, waiting your arrival.

Dol. If she comes back don't let her in. Tell her to come to-morrow morning. I cannot attend to any more business before court. [*He busies himself among papers.*]

Cor. [*Bows.*] I fly! [**Exit** *D. R. 4 E.*]

Dol. Egad! Some people must think lawyers are made of iron and work like machines! No! I'll listen to no more cases before court. I've only got one head and one pair of arms. [CORIOLANUS *puts his head in D. R. 4 E.* To CORIOLANUS.] Well, sir! What now?

Cor. [Enters.] She's come back! I delivered your message. She wrung her hands and said she came eighteen miles to see you, and she must return at noon.

Dol. I can't help it! She must come another time. I positively decline to see any one before court.

Cor. I quicken! [Exit *D. R. 4 E.*]

Dol. Some one without money to try to enlist my sympathies in helping some scalawag out of trouble. Not long ago I defended a tramp whom I thought unjustly used. I helped him out of the scrape and gave him a bowl of soup and some alms to help him on—and how did the rascal serve me? He published it about the town, and for two weeks I had every tramp from fifty miles around at my door begging for soup and alms. You don't get George Washington Dollerclutch in such a scrape again. [*Sees newspaper.*] Hello! what's this? [*Picks up paper and adjusts spectacles. Reads.*] "On the Brink of a Civil War." Lord bless us! [*Adjusts his glasses.*] "Slavery and Anti-Slavery." "The Inauguration of Lincoln." Ah! That's my man—Old honest Abe! He'll show those rascally slave masters a thing or two before he's done with them. [*Reads.*] "Firing on Fort Sumter." "Major Ander—" [*Drops paper.*] Hang it all! I can't get that girl out of my mind. What the dickens did she want to say that for, anyhow? [*Sighs.*] Well! Well! [*Picks up paper and reads.*] "Major Anderson with seventy men, after a brave resistance of three hours against five thousand Secessionists, was finally obliged to surrender." Eighteen miles to see me? It must be an important case. [*Rises to his feet.*] Confound it anyhow! Why did I let it slip? [*Calls.*] Coriolanus!

Enter CORIOLANUS, *D. R.* 4 *E.*

Cor. You have called! I have obeyed your summons.

Dol. Hold your tongue! Just go at once, and run after that girl and bring her back.

Cor. [*Bows.*] I quicken! [**Exit** *D. R.* 4 *E.*]

Dol. Why the dickens does she want to come here and upset my peace of mind?

Enter CORIOLANUS, *D. R.* 4 *E. He goes to R. C.* DOLLERCLUTCH *C.*

Cor. In compliance with your desire, I have brought her back and left her on the door-step.

Dol. You thundering blockhead! Why didn't you bring her up here? Why the devil did you send her away in the first place? Here I'm losing all this valuable time. Usher her up at once.

Cor. I quicken! [**Exit** CORIOLANUS, *D. R.* 4 *E.* DOLLERCLUTCH *busies himself among his papers.*]

Dol. Perhaps she's a fine rich lady, and I'll have a fat case. If not, I'll have nothing to do with her. I'll hustle her off in short order. I'll crush her with a look.

Enter CORIOLANUS, *D. R.* 4 *E.*, *bowing in* HILDA.

Dol. [*Aside, looking at* HILDA.] H'm! No money in her case. I'll have nothing to do with it!

Cor. [*At D. R.* 4 *E.*] My mission I've fulfilled; your pleasure I await.

Dol. [*To* CORIOLANUS.] Get out! Didn't I tell you not to let me be disturbed before court?

Cor. I'll make an honorable retreat. [**Exit** *D. R.* 4 *E.*]

Hil. [*C.*] I beg your pardon, sir! Are you not Mr. Dollerclutch, the lawyer?

Dol. Now, ain't you ashamed of yourself hanging around a gentleman's door and carrying on in such an outlandish manner, when I'm so busy, eh?

Hil. I am very sorry, sir, but—but—

Dol. But what?

Hil. Oh, sir! I—I—

Dol. It's no use! It'll cost you two hundred dollars to look at me. Take my advice and go home and leave law alone. I dismiss the case. I'll not charge you a cent for that advice. Don't you say another word—good day! [*Waves his hand. He busies himself among his papers.* HILDA *wrings her hands. After a pause.*] Well, why don't you say something? What's your name?

Hil. Hilda Wallace, sir!

Dol. Humph! Trying to raise a subscription for an able-bodied invalid, I suppose?

Hil. Oh, no, sir! I come to see if you could not help a poor girl out of a sad trouble.

Dol. [*Aside.*] I thought so! Trying to work the sympathetic dodge. [*To* HILDA.] What! Do you want to get a divorce?

Hil. No, sir! I came to see if you could find out who my parents are, and, also, whether I am married or not.

Dol. Lord, bless us! The girl must be crazy!

Hil. [*At desk.*] Oh, sir! just listen to my story, and I know that you will be able to help me in this, my sore trouble.

Dol. [*Crosses to R., pulls forward two chairs, and motions* HILDA *to be seated.*] Well, well! go on! [*Aside.*] There's the morning's court business, and not a thing done. [HILDA *sits L. C.* DOLLERCLUTCH *R. C.*]

Hil. I was brought up by a family named Wallace, who live in Norfolk, Virginia, and I supposed that I was their daughter, until a discovery I made two years ago convinced me that I was not.

Dol. [*Getting interested.*] And what discovery did you make?

Hil. [*Unfolding a package.*] I found this dress hidden away in one of the bureau drawers. [*Hands it to him.*]

Dol. Lord, bless me! Why, it's a baby dress.

Hil. Yes, sir! and when I made inquiries about it I learned that it was one I wore when a child.

Dol. Well, there was nothing strange about that?

Hil. No, sir! But on examination, I found these initials, A. M., which you see worked in it!

Dol. Ah! yes! Precisely!

Hil. And when I called their attention to it they seemed confused and did not know what to reply. I kept the dress, determined to find out more, if I could!

Dol. And you did?

Hil. No, sir! but I learned since that the man I married could unveil the mystery which shrouds my birth.

Dol. And won't he enlighten you?

Hil. No, sir! all my attempts have proved futile.

Dol. But did you not say that this man was your husband?

Hil. Yes, sir! But he must have some object in keeping my identity secret.

Dol. But how did you become acquainted with this man, and how did you come to marry him?

Hil. He was a regular visitor at our home, and I noticed on many occasions that he paid Mrs. Wallace money. However, I fell desperately in love with him, and when he proposed that we get married, I, of course, was only too happy to consent.

Dol. And his name?

Hil. Ralph Murdell!

Dol. Ralph Murdell! Humph! I don't like the name —got a bad sound to it.

Hil. He took me to a little village in the suburbs about four miles from Norfolk, where we were married in a little chapel by an old country preacher.

Dol. And you were happy, I suppose?

Hil. Yes, until about two weeks later, when he was about to leave me. He said he had to go North to attend to some business. I would not listen to it, unless he took me with him.

Dol. That's right, my girl! And he took you, of course?

Hil. Yes; but it was on condition that I should keep the marriage a secret, and not recognize him in the presence of others.

Dol. And what the deuce was that for?

Hil. He said his family were very proud, and he wanted to gain their consent before he made our marriage public.

Dol. Oh, the rascal! And you listened to him?

Hil. Yes, sir! To my sorrow, I did. He recommended me to a young lady who wanted a lady's maid. I accepted the position on his assurance that he would soon claim me before the world as his wife.

Dol. And who is this lady with whom you now are?

Hil. Adrienne Lowville!

Dol. What! The daughter of Wm. Lowville, who owns Beachwood, eighteen miles from here, on the Essex road?

Hil. Oh, yes, sir! Do you know him?

Dol. Well, I'd like to know who don't! Got a railroad in each pocket. But, about your husband—is he acquainted there?

Hil. Alas! yes! He is a constant visitor, and I more than suspect that his attentions to my mistress imply more than he wishes me to believe.

Dol. [*Throws baby dress on table, R. 3 E.*] Oh! That's his game, is it? A case of throwing you over for her, eh?

Hil. I fear so, sir; for she is madly in love with him, and thinks him a saint. When I called him to account for his actions, he laughed at me. He then informed me that he would do as he pleased, and that I was not his wife at all; that ours was a mock marriage.

Dol. [*Jumps up.*] The deuce he did! Oh, the villain, to take advantage of a poor innocent girl.

Hil. [*Rises.*] Oh, sir! but it was legal—it—

Dol. [DOLLERCLUTCH *L. C.*, HILDA *R. C.*] Have you got your marriage certificate?

Hil. No, sir! I never thought of that, sir.

Dol. Then, what proof have you?

Hil. Alas, none! But, oh sir! can't you investigate it? There surely must be a record kept of all marriages. Can't you get a copy of the church register, where it must have been entered?

Dol. That's so! I never thought of that! But, my dear girl, that will be a difficult matter, now that the country is in a *furore* and on the verge of a civil war; and it will cost money to do it, my dear girl; money.

Hil. [*Crosses to desk L. 3 E.*] Oh, sir! I thought of that! Here are twelve dollars that I saved out of my scanty earnings. Won't it be enough, sir?

Dol. [*Up C.*] Enough? Why, it wouldn't pay for dipping a pen into the ink, to say nothing about the trouble of licking a postage stamp.

Hil. [*Sobs.*] What shall I do—what shall I do?

Dol. [*Taking out handkerchief.*] Take up that money and put it in your pocket immediately! I'll not take a cent of it. I never was so insulted in my life. [*Crosses to R.*]

Hil. [*C.*] Oh, won't you help me out of my trouble?

Dol. Help you? Of course I will! Who said I wouldn't? Do you think I'll stand by and see an innocent girl wronged in this manner? No! I'll see this thing through, if it costs me a fortune! Oh, the villain! [DOLLERCLUTCH *at desk,* HILDA *at table R. 2 E.*]

Enter CORIOLANUS, *D. R. 4 E., with lunch.*

Cor. Your lunch, sir! [*Puts it on desk.*]

Dol. D—n the lunch! Get out!

Cor. I quicken! [**Exit** *D. C.* HILDA *sobs. She picks up baby dress from table.*]

Dol. [*Down C.*] What are you crying about?

Hil. I am so grateful to you, sir, for taking a poor girl's trouble to heart.

Dol. Now, don't you be deluding yourself with any such idea. This is business, I tell you; business. What do you know about business, I'd like to know?

Hil. I beg your pardon, sir!

Dol. Why do you come and arouse my sympathetic heart, and upset all my court business?

Hil. Can I do aught, sir?

Dol. No—yes—that is—shut up! Give me that dress! Now, you go back and don't let that husband of yours suspect anything. [*Puts on his hat, etc.* DOLLERCLUTCH *at desk,* HILDA *C.*]

Hil. Are you going out, sir?

Dol. Hold your tongue! This is the way I prepare myself for court business; and there's my nice lunch, too! [*Stuffs baby dress in his bosom, leaving a part sticking out.*] Now, go home and don't bother me till you hear from me. I'm going to take the first train for Norfolk!

By Force of Impulse.   21

Enter CORIOLANUS *at door C.*

Cor. It's time to go to court!

Dol. D—n the court! I'll see this thing through. [*He bolts for the C. door and upsets* CORIOLANUS *in his haste to get out.* **Exit** *through C. door.*]

Cor. The court is sitting! [CORIOLANUS *C.*, HILDA *L. C. Whistle scene.*]

Scene 2: WOOD-PASS IN THE NEIGHBORHOOD OF WILLIAM LOWVILLE'S RESIDENCE AT BEACHWOOD.

Enter HENRY LOWVILLE, *R. 2 E., with gun resting on arm.*

Hen. [*Looking off L. E.*] The guests are beginning to arrive, and I suppose I must, as a member of the family, be on hand and help do the honors of entertaining the motley crowd. [*Sighs.*] Ah! how I hate the hollow mockery of fashionable society—how I hate to mingle in the giddy deception hidden under the guise of polite gentility—bah!

Enter REGINALD, *L. 2 E.*

Reg. Why, how now, Henry! One of your melancholy fits again? Ha! ha! ha! [*Shakes hands.*]

Hen. Yes, confoundedly so! I've got the blues with a vengeance.

Reg. Come, come, old fellow, shake off this feeling. Why, you look as if you had buried your best friend. Come, have a weed! [*Offers segar case.*] Nothing like a smoke, you know, to calm a perturbed mind.

Hen. [*Lights segar.*] Yes, there is a certain soothing influence about it; that's a fact.

Reg. Ah! now you look more like yourself. But how is this—why are you not at your post, doing the honors to the guests?

Hen. Because I hate these empty shows. What are all these receptions but one maze of dissipation, where everybody seems to outdo the other in silliness?

Reg. I agree with you there, Henry. There are many sins and much hypocrisy and deceit practiced under the veil of studied politeness, and the sacred bond of friendship becomes a mere matter of form to further the ends of frivolous and sordid desires.

Hen. And the women! All deception, heartless, fickle. Show me a woman in this gilded age of fashion devoid of fashion's impress—devoid of—

Reg. Nay, Henry! You are prejudiced—all women are not so. There are still many who possess all the noble attributes that Heaven instilled in her heart, that make her all that is beautiful and endearing in the eyes of a true man.

Hen. Yes; but artificial show has supplanted her—I know not the ideal.

Reg. Aye! but I know one.

Hen. And she is—

Reg. Your sister Adrienne!

Hen. Oho! I understand. Ha! ha! ha! Well, well, there's my hand on it. I give in. There is no one in the wide world that I would be more pleased to call brother.

Reg. [*Confused.*] You misunderstand—you—

Hen. Well, well; so be it. But I had better go up to the mansion and make the guests comfortable, and help Adrienne complete the arrangements for the grand ball this evening. Will you come? [*Crosses to L.* REGINALD *to R.*]

Reg. Not just at present. I want to have a little quiet stroll in these grand old woods; besides, I want to finish my weed.

Hen. Well, I'm off! [**Exit** *L. 2 E.*]

Reg. As good a fellow as ever lived; with a tinge of melancholy in his make-up, and a little bitter against the female sex in general. Heigho! Probably a victim of a heartless coquette. Hum! That awkward slip of the tongue has betrayed me. He has discovered my feelings toward Adrienne. [*Leans against tree, L. 2 E., in a study.*]

Enter SAMMY DEWDROP *and* ADOLPHUS SOFTHEAD, *R. 2 E. They do not perceive* REGINALD.

Sammy. [*C.*] Hang it all if I don't think we've lost the way! [*Looks around.*]

Adolphus. [*R. C.*] Why didn't you listen to me and come by the regular road? Oh, Sammy! What if night should overtake us? Oh! oh! [SAMMY *scratches his head.* REGINALD *perceives them.*]

Reg. [*Aside.*] Two big school-boys!

Sam. Now, look a'here, Adolphus! How did I know we'd get in such a pickle? [*Sees sign on tree R. F.*] Hurrah! We're all right! Here's a finger-post! [SAMMY *R. C.* ADOLPHUS *C. Reads :*] "Beware!" [ADOLPHUS *jumps in terror.*] "Do not disturb the deer." Oh, pshaw! What shall we do?

Adol. I wish I'd stayed home!

Sam. It was all your fault that we came. You said there would be lots of nice girls there, and we should be sure to fall in love with ever so many.

Reg. Ha! ha! ha!

Adol. [*Scared.*] Oh! oh!

Sam. [*Clutches* ADOLPHUS *fearfully.*] What was that?

Reg. [*Comes forward, smiling.* ADOLPHUS *R. C.* SAMMY *C.* REGINALD *L. C.*] Gentlemen, you seem distressed. Can I serve you?

Sam. [*Brightens up suddenly.* *To* ADOLPHUS.] Oh! you coward, to get frightened like that! Why can't you be brave like me?

Adol. You were just as afraid as I was.

Reg. [*Laughs.*] Have a smoke? [*Offers cigar-case to* SAMMY.] It will help to quiet your nerves.

Adol. [*To* SAMMY, *aside.*] Oh, Lucifer! I never smoked in my life.

Sam. Neither did I! But we must take one, you know; it isn't polite to refuse—besides, all men smoke.

Adol. Black as ink! Strong as old Nick, I bet.

Reg. You seem to have lost your way.

Sam. We were on our way to Holly Mansion, when we lost our way in this confounded jungle.

Reg. Ah! Then I can be of service to you. That is my destination, also, and if agreeable, I shall be most happy to guide you. [*With mock politeness.* SAMMY *and* ADOLPHUS *both try to shake hands with* REGINALD *at once. They both speak together.*]

Sam. You're a trump

Adol. Put it there, old boy!

Reg. This way, gentlemen! [**Exeunt,** *L. 2 E. Whistle scene.*]

Scene 3: GARDEN ADJOINING WM. LOWVILLE'S MANSION.

Enter ANASTASIA MAITLAND, *and* CORIOLANUS *with valise, L.* 2 *E.*

Anastasia. Well, I never! Not a soul about to receive me. And after all that jaunt from the station, too. I declare it's an outrage. They could have sent their carriage to the station for me, to say the least. If there was somebody about, I should feel inclined to faint. [*Sits on bench, L.* 3 *E.*] Coriolanus!

Cor. [*At R. C. Bows stiffly.*] Your pleasure, madam!

Anas. Get my smelling-bottle out of the valise—be quick!

Cor. [*Puts down valise.*] I quicken!

Anas. And there's Reginald; why was he not at the station? He knew I was coming. [CORIOLANUS *hands smelling-bottle.*] Won't I give him a piece of my mind! [*Music heard at distance.*] Well, I declare. [*Rises.*] If they haven't commenced dancing already! Coriolanus, go at once and announce my arrival.

Cor. Madam, I obey! I will go in advance and have the servants to announce us. [**Exit** *R. 2 E.*]

Anas. Announce *us!* Did I ever see such impudence —announce *us!* Just as if *he*, a common servant, was such a distinguished personage as I am. Oh! it's disgusting! [**Exit** *R. 2 E.*]

Enter ADRIENNE *and* HILDA, *R. 4 E.*

Adrienne. Did you arrange the flowers on the table, as I desired?

Hil. Yes, my lady!

Adri. [*Sits on bench, R. 3 E.*] What a beautiful evening! All nature seems hushed, as if it had gone to sleep on the broad bosom of the day. [*Sighs.*] Hilda, were you ever in love?

Hil. [*Standing L. of bench.*] Yes—no—that is, I—I—

Adri. [*Laughs.*] Why, you silly little goose. You act as if it were a crime to be in love. You tremble like a leaf.

Hil. I—I am cold. The night air is chilly. If you'll excuse me, I will go in and get a shawl.

Adri. Oh, certainly. [HILDA *is about to go.*] Hilda, when you go in, peep into the parlor and see if Ralph—I mean, Mr. Murdell, has arrived.

Hil. Yes, madam! [*R. C. Aside.*] She loves him; she cannot hide it. [**Exit** *R. 3 E.*]

Adri. He is late! What can detain him? He begged for the honor of the first dance. The third has already been danced and he is not here. Oh! how slowly the minutes glide. Ah! he comes at last.

Enter RALPH, *L. 2 E.*

Ralph. [*L. of bench.*] This is an unexpected pleasure!
Adri. Truant sir! This is punctuality!
Ralph. Allow me to offer my humblest apologies for my offense, and if a life's devotion could repay it, command me.
Adri. Still the disappointment would remain.
Ralph. Then you were disappointed, Miss Lowville? Adrienne! [*Takes her hand.*]
Adri. Certainly! [*Withdraws her hand.*] Why shouldn't I be when I was debarred from the pleasure of the first dance, simply because it was pledged to one who did not fulfill his promise? [*Music heard.*] Hark! That's the quadrille I have given to Mr. Maitland. [*About to go to R.*]
Ralph. [*Takes her hand and gently forces her to bench.*] Nay, Adrienne! Do not go.
Adri. And would you have me be a truant like you? [*They sit.*]
Ralph. Yes, because I cannot let you go. Adrienne, long have I sought for such an opportunity [**Enter** HILDA *R. 4 E.*] to pour into your ears the passion that is consuming me.
Adri. Ralph, hush! Some one approaches.
Hil. [*Comes forward C.*] Madam! Mr. Maitland was inquiring for you for this quadrille.

By Force of Impulse.   27

Adri. I almost forgot it. [*Aside to* RALPH.]   I'll be back presently.   [*To* HILDA.]   Come, Hilda! [*Both* Exeunt *R.* 2 *E.* RALPH Exits *L.* 2 *E.*]

Enter SAMMY *and* ADOLPHUS, *L.* 2 *E.*

Sam. [*Looking after the girls.*]   Did you see her? Oh, what a heavenly being! My heart goes after her, and I guess I'll follow my heart. [*About to rush after.* ADOLPHUS *pulls him back.*]

Adol. No you don't! If anybody goes, it's me. [*About to go.* SAMMY *pulls him back.*]

Sam. I want to pour my heart in her ear!

Adol. And I want to let my soul mingle with hers!

Sam. Well, we can't both make love to her at once. I have it! We'll draw lots! [*Pulls matches from pocket.*] Who draws the short stick proposes first, and if she refuses the short stick then the long stick will have a chance.

Adol. Oh, Sammy! What a head you've got.

Sam [*Holds sticks towards* ADOLPHUS.] Draw! [ADOLPHUS *draws long stick.*]

Adol. Just my luck!

Sam. Ah! Now, Dolphy, I'll show you how to do it. Hush! She's coming back! Now you hide behind there. [*Pointing* ADOLPHUS *hides behind flower urn, C.*]

Enter ADRIENNE, *R.* 2 *E.*   SAMMY *falls on his knee.*

Sam. Most adorable angel, whose liquid eyes do penetrate the inmost depths of my entranced soul, listen to one who has loved you from his childhood. Fill me with ecstasy by the avowal from thy honeyed lips that you will be forever mine.

Adri. [*Laughs heartily.*] Rise, you foolish boy, and go home and tell your mother to put a mustard draft on your feet and give you a dose of paregoric.

Sam. [*Gets up and scratches his head.*] Squashed, by Jupiter! [*He walks to L.*]
Adri. [*R. Aside.*] Where is Ralph, I wonder!
Adol. [*Coming forward, C. To* SAMMY.] Go home, you foolish boy, and get some paregoric and let Adolphus take off the prize. [ADRIENNE *turns.* ADOLPHUS *falls on his knee.*]
Adri. Another proposal?
Adol. Fairest of the fair and fairer yet, take this my heart and do with it what you like. It's yours forevermore. [**Enter** REGINALD, *R. 2 E., who takes* ADRIENNE'S *place.* ADRIENNE *R.*, REGINALD *R. C.*, ADOLPHUS *C.*, SAMMY *L.*] Play with it, use it for a foot-ball—do with it what you like, as long as you take your true Adolphus with it. My father owns sixty-eight brick houses, twenty race horses, three hundred slaves, and one-quarter of an acre of good farming land—besides—[*Discovers he is talking to* REGINALD.] The devil! [*Starts and rushes off L. 2 E.* SAMMY *runs after him.*]
Sam. Who had better take paregoric now? [**Exit** *L. 2 E.* ADRIENNE *and* REGINALD *laugh.*]
Reg. Two foolish, overgrown boys, whose mental powers have not kept pace with their physical. Pray be seated, Miss Lowville. [ADRIENNE *sits, bench R. 3 E.* REGINALD *remains standing.*]
Adri. Mr. Maitland, I owe you an apology. I promised you a quadrille, but I regret having disappointed you.
Reg. Don't mention it. I willingly submit to the disappointment, since it has afforded me the pleasure of enjoying a few moments' quiet conversation with one whose amiable disposition and lofty sentiments command my profoundest respect and admiration.
Adri. You flatter me, sir!
Reg. Nay, Miss Lowville, believe me, I am sincere. I have watched the development of noble traits, the unfold-

ing of a noble character prompted by a pure and loving heart; the expression of high and lofty thought—all of which impressions have sunk so deeply into my being that they seem a part of myself. Miss Lowville, I use no honeyed words, but I offer you the heart and hand of an honest man, who will love, honor and shield you through all the walks of life.

Adri. [*Rises.*] Mr. Maitland, you honor me with the offer of such a noble heart as yours, and could I accept it, I should be proud to wear it in my bosom. Such noble love requires a noble love in return. But I cannot.

Reg. Perhaps—in time—

Adri. Alas! I cannot give you hope. But friends we shall ever be. [REGINALD *turns away.*] Will you accept the hand of friendship?

Reg. Yes! Yes! Pardon me! Friends we shall always be. [**Exit** ADRIENNE, *R. 2 E.*]

Enter CORIOLANUS, *R. 4 E.*

Cor. Sir Reginald, your honored aunt awaits your coming in the conservatory.

Reg. I will attend her immediately. [**Exit** REGINALD, *R. 2 E.*]

Cor. [*Coming down C.*] Coriolanus, I am proud of you—you have acquitted yourself nobly—you have made an impression upon her maiden heart, I feel assured. She recognizes the true nobility that is hidden under the garb of the menial. How I hate these clothes! Oh! Anastasia, thou knowest true worth when thou see'st it. [*Walks to right.*]

Enter DOLLERCLUTCH, *L. 4 E. Comes down C.*

Dol. Well, I've got here at last, and if I can only manage to meet Hilda. But how shall I contrive to see her?

[*Looks around and sees* CORIOLANUS.] Ah! there's one of the servants! I'll question him. [*To* CORIOLANUS.] Hey, there, you clown! Come here. [CORIOLANUS *turns.*] Coriolanus, by all that is wonderful. Well, this is particularly gratifying. But, how is it that I find you here? Have you left the other place?

Cor. I am a visitor here! I have escorted Miss Maitland to the grand reception.

Dol. Oh! I thought you were going to say you owned this place. However, you are just the person to do me a little service. Run to the mansion and tell Miss Lowville's maid to step out here a moment, that a gentleman wishes to speak to her. [CORIOLANUS *about to go in high dudgeon.*] Hold on! That won't do—it will attract attention—a few lines will be better. [*Pulls out tablet and writes.*]

Cor. [*Aside.*] I'm no common servant! Such impudence, to ask a gentleman like me. No, thank you! [**Exit** *in high dudgeon, R. 2 E.*]

Dol. There, I guess that will do! [*Folding up note.*]

Enter ANASTASIA, *R. 2 E.*

Dol. Here, you clown, take this note and mind—

Anas. Sir!

Dol. The devil! [*Aside.*] Where did that infernal rascal get to! [*To* ANASTASIA.] I beg a million pardons, madam! [*Aside.*] Confound that rascal! [*To* ANASTASIA.] Pray pardon me, madam—a mistake, I assure you—mistook you for another.

Anas. Oh!

Dol. [*L. Aside.*] What an amiable creature!

Anas. [*R. Aside.*] What a charming personage, and so very polite—Hem!

Dol. Did you speak, madam?

Anas. Such a beautiful evening!

Enter RALPH, *L. 4 E. He pauses at C.*

Dol. Why, yes! and doubly so since the arrival of such charming simplicity.

Ralph. Ha! ha! ha! [*Comes down C.* ANASTASIA *and* DOLLERCLUTCH *are startled.* ANASTASIA **Exits** *R. 2 E., with great dignity.*]

Dol. [*L.*] Were you laughing at me, sir?

Ralph. Yes! at the picture of charming simplicity. Ha! ha! ha!

Dol. Hem! perhaps your name is Paul Pry?

Ralph. Perhaps it is! [*With a shrug.*] If you have any grievance, there's my card. [*Hands him card, and is about to go.*]

Dol. [*Looks at card. Aside.*] Ralph Murdell?—the devil! [*To* RALPH.] Well, I thought you were either a Paul Pry or a villainous rascal!

Ralph. [*Turns suddenly.*] What did you say?

Dol. I say we are often mistaken. [*Crosses to R. Aside.*] I'll keep my eyes on you, my fine bird. [**Exit** *R. 2 E.*]

Ralph. [*Looking around.*] Where is Hilda? I did not like the look in her eye! I must be careful, or she will upset all my plans. She comes.

Enter HILDA, *R. 2 E.*

Ralph. You are late!

Hil. I am, sir! but not too late for what I have to say. Think you I will stand calmly by and witness your villainy and allow you to deceive another as you have basely deceived me? No! If I am not your wife in law, I am in the sight of Heaven, and I dare you to make another victim.

Ralph. [*L., aside.*] I must pacify her somehow. [*To* HILDA.] Hilda! [*Takes her hand and leads her to bench*

L. 3 E. **Enter** ADRIENNE *in` background R. 5 E. She listens behind statue L. 4 E.*] I have repented saying those harsh words. I did not mean it. It was in anger I spoke.

Hil. Oh, Ralph! if I could only believe you.

Ralph. You can; and if you could but look into my heart you would know that you, and you only, are the one for whom its pulses beat.

Enter REGINALD *and* ANASTASIA *R. 2 E.* ADRIENNE *comes down C. majestically.* RALPH *and* HILDA *rise.* ANASTASIA *R.*, REGINALD *R. C.*, ADRIENNE *C.*, RALPH *L. C.*, HILDA *L.*

Adri. Reginald Maitland, you offered me your heart and hand and I refused. I have reconsidered my refusal. If you still honor me with the offer, I accept. [**Tableau.** **Enter** *all quickly.* DOLLERCLUTCH, *R. 3 E.* CORIOLANUS, *R. 2 E.* SAMMY *and* ADOLPHUS, *L. 3 E.* HILDA *and* ANASTASIA *faint.* ANASTASIA *falls into the arms of* DOLLERCLUTCH. CORIOLANUS *looks on with envy.* SAMMY *and* ADOLPHUS *try to support* HILDA. *Comic business.* REGINALD *accepts* ADRIENNE'S *hand eagerly.* ADRIENNE, *with heaving bosom, majestically defiant to* RALPH. RALPH *disconcerted.*]

	REG.	ADRI.	
	DOLLER.		RALPH.
	ANAS.		SAM., ADOL.
	CORIO.		HILDA.
R.			*L.*
		C.	

Quick Curtain.

ACT II.

Scene 1 : SITTING ROOM OF THE MAITLAND COTTAGE.

ANASTASIA *discovered knitting, seated at table, L. C.* CORIO-
LANUS *at door, R. 3 E.*

Anas. Coriolanus, have you ordered the carriage to the station ?

Corio. Your orders have been obeyed, madam ! [*With bow. Crosses to C.*]

Anas. Then everything is in readiness for the reception of the bride and groom. You may retire, Coriolanus, and be pleased to announce them as soon as they arrive.

Corio. I will hold myself in readiness to gratify your desires. [*Going, aside.*] The darling creature ! She cannot trust her feelings when alone in my presence. Every look, every action, speak of the great admiration she has for me.

Anas. Well ! [*Impatiently.*] Will you go?

Corio. I quicken ! [**Exit** *D. R. 3 E.*]

Anas. The stupid dolt, with his stuck-up manners. I hate him ! I wonder whether Mary has attended to the room. [*Goes to door, L. 2 E., and calls.*] Mary ! Mary ! [MARY *answers off entrance,* "Ma'am."] Have you thoroughly aired Reginald's apartments? [MARY, *as before,* "Yes, Ma'am." ANASTASIA *closes door.*] So ! Reginald and his bride will soon be here, and they will find everything well regulated, thanks to my personal supervision. I can't say that I like Reginald's choice. The bold thing, to throw herself upon a man like that, and before everybody, too! It's outrageous—not a bit of maidenly modesty—I shall hate her, I know I shall. And Reginald was so pleased to accept the proud thing. What fools men are! Well, well; I hope the dear boy will not be disappointed in her and live unhappily. [*She sighs heavily and resumes knitting.*] What a strange thing love is, to be sure. Who could that stranger have been I met in the garden—such a splendid man! So full of good sense! So polite! Oh, perfectly lovely! I could fall in love with such a dear man. [**Enter** MORRIS MAITLAND, *D. R. 2 E.*] I—— Morris!

Mor. [*C*] Not yet arrived? H'm! The train must be late. Has the carriage gone?

Anas. Yes, brother! I gave Coriolanus strict orders to attend to it!

Mor. Well, I suppose they will get here in good time. But it's getting late—past nine o'clock. [*At table, L. C.*] Sister, you will do all in your power to make Reginald's wife comfortable and receive her with the respect due the wife of my honored son.

Anas. I will do my part, Morris, provided she does hers. But I'm afraid Reginald has made a poor choice.

Mor. Sister, you are prejudiced. Reginald is an honest, sensible and dutiful son. Although her connections are very aristocratic, more so, in fact, than I could cordially approve, yet, I have faith in him to believe that his choice has been wise, and that she will prove an honor to my son and the pride of his father's heart.

Anas. Well, I have no more to say. I hope that she will fulfill your expectations.

Mor. She is now my daughter and shall receive a hearty welcome into the bosom of our family.

Enter CORIOLANUS, *D. R. 3 E.*

Corio. Reginald and Adrienne Maitland! [MORRIS *at L. C.*; ANASTASIA *rises and goes to fireplace, L. 3 E.*]

Enter REGINALD, ADRIENNE *and* HILDA, *D. R. 3 E.* HILDA, *R.*, ADRIENNE, *R. C.*, REGINALD, *C.*, MORRIS, *L. C.*, ANASTASIA, *L.*

Mor. [*Embracing* REGINALD.] My son! welcome to your paternal home.

Reg. Father, allow me to bring to you a daughter, my wife. [*Leads her to him, then crosses to shake hands with* ANASTASIA.]

Mor. My daughter, welcome to our humble home—receive the blessing of—

Adri. [*Coldly.*] Thanks! You honor me. [*Crosses to L.*] Reginald, [*wearily*] I am tired. [MORRIS *retreats painfully.* ANASTASIA *exchanges looks with him and draws herself loftily erect.*]

Reg. Adrienne, my aunt—Miss Maitland.

Adri. [*Bows haughtily.*] We've met before. [*To* REGINALD.] Conduct me to my room. [REGINALD *bows.* **Exeunt** ADRIENNE *and* REGINALD, *D. L. 2 E.* HILDA *follows with wraps, etc.* MORRIS *crosses to R. Sinks in armchair R. of table.*]

Anas. H'm! I thought so! An iceberg. Proud and dignified. Above such humble surroundings! Brother!

Mor. My son! my son!

Anas. Did I not tell you? Perhaps you'll give me credit in the future for a little sense.

Mor. [*Sternly.*] Anastasia! Leave me.

Anas. Well, you needn't bite my head off because I spoke the truth. [**Exit** *in dudgeon, D. R. 3 E.*]

Mor. My fondest expectations blighted. Heaven grant they will be happy! but—[*shakes his head*] I doubt it—I doubt it.

Enter REGINALD, *D. L. 2 E.* *He approaches table slowly.*
MORRIS *rises and turns away.*

Reg. Father!

Mor. [*Turns suddenly and embraces him.*] Oh, my son! I had such hopes for your future happiness! But alas!

Reg. Why, father, can you for a moment doubt it? [MORRIS *shakes his head.*] Adrienne is fatigued—worn out—weary from travel. Our journey has been extensive. In the morning she will be herself again.

Mor. I sincerely hope so, my son! but I fear you have made a great mistake. You may have loved well, but I fear too unwisely.

Reg. Father, you are mistaken in Adrienne. She is all that is noble—as free from deceit and the taint of the world as a child unborn. No, no, father! she is all that an honorable man could wish.

Mor. For your sake, I wish I could think as you do, but I cannot. Did she love you as a wife should, she would honor her husband so much as to show her respect, at least, to his father.

Reg. You had a right to expect a warmer acknowledgment of your welcome. But consider her fatigue. Time will command the respect and love due her husband's father.

Mor. Love is a spontaneous outburst of the heart. It is not of gradual growth. It takes not time to discover true innate worth in a person. Love detects it at a glance, and time only confirms the first impression. My son, is she all that you desire?

Reg. Yes, father, all.

Mor. And are you sure that she loves you?

Reg. [*Confused.*] Yes, father—that is—I—

Mor. Why this confusion?

Reg. I think she does.

Mor. Think? Why, did she not tell you as much?

Reg. Father, we will not discuss this subject any further. Suffice it to say that she is my wife, and I have sworn to love and honor her till death do us part, and I will do my duty, sir!

Mor. So be it, my son! and may Providence, who watches over us all, grant you a happy life. Heaven bless you, my son! [*Clock strikes.*] The hour for retiring is at hand. You will call your wife to attend our usual family devotion in the library ere retiring for the night.

Reg. I attend your pleasure! [**Exit** *D. L. 2 E.* MORRIS *strikes bell on table.*]

Enter ANASTASIA, *followed by* CORIOLANUS, *D. R. 3 E.* CORIOLANUS *R.*, ANASTASIA *C.*, MORRIS *L.*

Anas. Shall I call Reginald's wife?
Mor. Reginald has gone to do so.
Anas. Oh!
Mor. Please retire to the library; I will follow shortly. [**Exit** ANASTASIA, *followed by* CORIOLANUS, *D. R. 3 E.*]

Enter REGINALD, *D. L. 2 E.* MORRIS *crosses to R. C.*

Reg. [*L. C.*] Father, Adrienne wishes to be excused; she is too tired!

Mor. My son, you know the laws of this house. All the members of the family must attend family prayer. This law has ever been kept inviolate by my ancestors, and it shall not be broken in this instance. You will inform your wife that I insist upon her attendance. [**Exit** REGINALD *D. L. 2 E.* MORRIS *walks the floor.*]

Enter ADRIENNE *quickly, D. L. 2 E., followed by* REGINALD. *She crosses to table, L. C.* MORRIS *R. C.*

Adri. Sir, in answer to your request, I asked to be excused; nevertheless, you insist upon a sacrifice of my own inclinations and desires. In this matter, I wish to inform you, I will suit my own pleasure. Good-night, sir! [*Going.*]

Mor. Madam, I respect your desires, and as the wife of my son, I honor you. But there are certain rules in this household from which there is no departure, and this is one. From time immemorial has this custom been a law at our fireside. As you are now a member of our family, I ask of you, [ADRIENNE *turns away*] nay, I beg of you, be not the first to violate this rule.

Adri. [*Haughtily.*] I refuse to comply!

Mor. [*Sternly.*] Then, madam, you compel me to assert my authority. As the master of this house, I insist upon your attendance at family prayer!

Adr. [*Drawing herself erect.*] Sir!

Reg. [*At fire-place.*] Father!

Mor. Nay! I command you!

Adri. [*To* REGINALD.] Will you stand by and allow this indignity?

Reg. Adrienne—I—

Mor. [*Crosses to D. R. 3 E.*] Enough! I await your presence in the library. [**Exit** *D. R. 3 E.* ADRIENNE *sinks into chair on R. of table.* REGINALD *in a pleading attitude. Whistle scene.*]

Scene 2: A STREET IN 1*st* GROOVES.

Enter RALPH, *L. 1 E.*

Ralph. Confound it, I cannot bear it any longer. This wandering around, nursing my wrath, is becoming unendurable. After having won her love, to be snatched from

By Force of Impulse. 39

me by that infernal Maitland—curse him!—and all through that she-devil, Hilda—curse them both! Oh! I could tear them to pieces!

Enter HENRY, *R. 1 E., in officer's uniform with paper in hand.* RALPH *turns away.*

Hen. [*Aside.*] Ralph Murdell! I never liked the looks of that man. [*To* RALPH.] Hello! Lost your tongue? [*R. C.*]

Ralph. [*C.*] No! but I lost something else!

Hen. Lost a love, perhaps?

Ralph. No! I've lost my temper!

Hen. [*Aside.*] Was spooney on Adrienne! [*To* RALPH.] Well, I'm glad you lost it!

Ralph. Glad I lost what?

Hen. Your temper.

Ralph. Oh! I didn't understand.

Hen. Why, if you *lost* your temper, you are well rid of it, and ought to be jolly. But you look as if you had it still. Ha! ha! ha!

Ralph. Confound your jokes; I'm in no humor for levity.

Hen. No, I guess not. But where have you kept yourself buried? I have not seen you since my sister's Grand Ball. I suppose you know she's married to Maitland?

Ralph. Yes! yes! I wish her much joy. What are you doing in that uniform?

Hen. Oh! I've enlisted in the army and was made a recruiting officer. There is going to be a hot time. The rebels have taken possession of all the prominent military stations in the South. And when Lincoln made a call for three hundred thousand volunteers, I could not resist the desire to do my duty and help preserve the Union. Besides, I was getting tired of the lazy, drone-like life of society.

Ralph. And are you seeking volunteers?

Hen. Yes; besides, I am looking up a lot of individuals whose names I have here.

Ralph. Volunteers?

Hen. No! The President has ordered a draft to be made for men, and I am on the look-out for some.

Ralph. Have you got me down in the draft?

Hen. No! You are one of the lucky ones!

Ralph. Indeed! But it would have pleased me if you had. Still, you can accept me as a volunteer.

Hen. [*Aside.*] H'm! his disappointment has made him desperate. [*To* RALPH.] You surprise me, Murdell—you have more patriotism than I gave you credit for.

Ralph. This sort of life is too tame for me. I long for excitement!

Hen. [*Hands him paper and pencil*] You will please sign here!

Ralph. [*Signs paper.*] And when shall I report for duty?

Hen. To-morrow morning at ten o'clock, at headquarters.

Ralph. All right! I'll go and make the necessary preparations. I shall be on hand. [**Exit** *R.* 1 *E.*]

Hen. [*Crosses to L.*] I'm glad Adrienne did not marry that chap, for I did think that she thought a great deal of him. But you can never tell anything about women. They never do what you think they will. However, I am more than pleased that things have turned out as they did. A better or truer man never lived than Reginald Maitland.

Enter SAMMY *and* ADOLPHUS *arm in arm,* R. 1 E. *They do not perceive* HENRY.

Sam. I for one am getting discouraged. I've proposed to twenty-three women in two weeks and been rejected twenty-three times. [HENRY *examines paper.*]

Adol. And I've been rejected as many times as I've proposed. If I only had the courage I'd drown myself.

Sam. And if I only had the chance I'd enlist. But come, let us drown our troubles in a glass of soda water. [*Going towards L.* 1 *E.*]

Hen. Halt! [SAMMY *and* ADOLPHUS *clutch each other in terror.*]

Sam.
Adol. } Oh! Oh! [ADOLPHUS *aud* SAMMY *C.* HENRY *L.*]

Hen. [*To* SAMMY.] Your name!

Sam. Sammy Dewdrop!

Hen. Right! [*To* ADOLPHUS.] And yours?

Adol. Adolphus Softhead!

Hen. Right again! Gentlemen, I am happy to inform you that you have been drafted! [SAMMY *and* ADOLPHUS *collapse, terror-stricken.*]

Adol. Oh! I shall die!

Sam. [*Trying to brace up, but shaking like a leaf.*] Why don't you take it bravely like me? [*To* ADOLPHUS.]

Adol. I can't. I'll never come back alive—I know I shan't.

Sam. [*Brightening up suddenly.*] I have it. Happy thought. [*To* HENRY.] But they won't take me—I am in the last stage of consumption. [*Coughs.*] And they don't take consumptives.

Adol. [*Eagerly.*] And I have got—[*Beckons* HENRY *to come nearer—he whispers in his ear.*]

Hen. Very well, gentlemen. If that is so, you are exempt. [SAMMY *and* ADOLPHUS *elated, about to go.*] Halt! You will first accompany me to headquarters, where you will be examined by the doctor; and then, if you are in the condition you say you are, you will be allowed to go. [SAMMY *and* ADOLPHUS *get weak in the knees.*]

Sam. [*To* ADOLPHUS.] It's no use, Dolphy, the jig's up!
Adol. Why was I born?
Hen. About face! Forward, march. [**Exeunt** *all L. 1 E. Whistle scene.*]

Scene 3: OUTSIDE OF THE MAITLAND COTTAGE.

Enter HILDA, *L. 2 E.*

Hil. Oh! what shall I do! my mistress is so unhappy. She is pining away day by day, and all for love for that worthless villain, Ralph. Oh, if I could only unburden my heart to her and tell her all! If she only knew how base he is she would not grieve so. Sometimes, when I see her silent despair, I feel tempted to tell her all. But I promised to keep silent until I heard from Mr. Dollerclutch. I fear he also has deserted me. Here comes my mistress! I will avoid her! I cannot witness her misery—my heart goes out to her. [**Exit** *R. 2 E.*]

Enter ADRIENNE, *L. 2 E. She is very pale. Sits on bench R. C.*

Adri. When will this torture end? Could I but recall the fatal words that doomed me to a loveless life! I can only blame my impulsive nature. I knew not what I did—I was mad—and I must suffer the bitter consequences. Oh, cruel, cruel fate! [*Her head sinks on her arm, which is resting on back of bench.*]

Enter MORRIS *from cottage on L.*

Mor. [*At L. C.*] Madam!

Adri. [*Starts and rises haughtily.*] Your pleasure, sir!
Mor. There is a matter I wish to speak to you about.
Adri. Proceed, sir!
Mor. It is about my son. [ADRIENNE *braces herself.*] Until your advent into our family all was peace and sunshine; but now all is mystery and clouds. And you, madam, are the cause of this condition of affairs. [ADRIENNE *presses her hand to her heart.*] I speak in behalf of my son. Since his marriage to you I have noted a change in him. There is something weighing heavily on his mind.
Adri. And has *he* sent you to plead his cause?
Mor. No, madam! He has defended you in every particular; he has tried to hide the true state of affairs. His sense of honor is so high that he would not listen to a word against your action. His vow at the altar is sacred to him; he would suffer anything without a murmur, and he will ever defend his wife from the sneers of the world.
Adri. Will you enlighten me, sir, as to the nature of my offense?
Mor. You have destroyed the happiness of my son's life. He cannot hide the disappointment of his honest heart from the searching gaze of a father.
Adri. Sir! It is best that we understand each other. I decline further to listen to your upbraidings. You have no right to question my actions. I forbid you ever to broach this subject again. The die is cast. I know my duty as a wife; and to my husband, and to him alone, will I hold myself accountable for my actions. [**Exit** *majestically L. 2 E.* MORRIS *looks after her.*]

Enter ANASTASIA, *R. 2 E.*

Anas. Brother Morris; I'll not put up with it any longer. Things are getting to be in a pretty strait when a person of

my standing must submit to such snubbing—yes, brother,
I repeat, *snubbing.*
    Mor. Don't bother me ! [**Exit** *into cottage.*]

        Enter DOLLERCLUTCH, *gate C.*

  Anas. [*Looking after* MORRIS, *angrily.*] Well, I never! another snub !
  Dol. [*Down R.*] Ahem !
  Anas. [*Turns suddenly.*] There's that sweet man again. [*She affects shyness.*]
  Dol. I beg your pardon, madam ! but allow me to express my pleasure in being so fortunate as to meet your lovely self under such auspicious circumstances.
  Anas. You flatter me !
  Dol. By no means, madam !—by no means. That is something I would not be guilty of. What I said came from the heart, madam—from the heart ! Do you understand?
  Anas. I think I do, sir ! [*Aside.*] Perfectly captivating !
  Dol. Allow me to conduct you to a seat, you are tired standing. [*He leads her to bench R. C. They sit at each end of bench and gradually move up closer to each other during the subsequent dialogue. Comic business.*]
  Anas. [*Aside.*] I believe he is going to propose ! If he does, I'll accept him on the instant.
  Dol. [*Fidgeting.*] Madam, I—I—really I have not the pleasure of your name.
  Anas. Anastasia Maitland, sir !
  Dol. Anastasia ! What a beautiful name !
  Anas. Thank you !
  Dol. And so appropriate to your charming self. It will always remind me of an angel.
  Anas. Did you ever see an angel ?

Dol. Yes, many a one--but they were all painted!

Anas. Oh! But I really forgot what you said your name was!

Dol. George Washington Dollerclutch, at your service, madam! You may call me Father of my Country Dollerclutch for short.

Anas. Such a grand name! It is so poetical!

Dol. [*Nudges up closer.*] Ahem!

Anas. [*Aside.*] The declaration is coming! I will fall in his arms as soon as he makes it.

Dol. Madam—I--I—[*Pulls out baby dress instead of handkerchief and wipes his face.*]

Anas. My heart goes pitti-di-pat! [*Sees baby dress.*] Oh! [*She turns away.*]

Dol. [*Notices it for the first time. Aside.*] Confound it! I thought I had my handkerchief. [*To* ANASTASIA.] I beg your pardon, madam! [*Puts it away and gets his handkerchief.* ANASTASIA *smiles sweetly and bows her head.*] Ahem! as I was going to say—

Enter CORIOLANUS, *L. 2 E.*

Dol. You are—you are—[*Sees* CORIOLANUS.] The devil! [*Starts up.* CORIOLANUS *holds himself proudly erect.* ANASTASIA **Exits** *with dignity into cottage.*]

Cor. [*Aside.*] A rival?

Dol. Playing the eavesdropper, eh! [*Aside.*] I'll bounce the rascal! [*Leaps upon him suddenly and runs him off R. 2 E.*] I'll teach you better manners. [*Walks down stage.*]

Enter HILDA, *R. 2 E.*

Dol. Don't come back or I'll—[*Sees* HILDA.] Oh!

Hil. [*Comes forward quickly.*] Oh, sir! You have come at last. What news have you—is it good or bad?

Dol. My dear child, I have both good and bad. I have searched the church register, but found no record of the marriage.

Hil. Alas! Then I have no hope. [*Sobs.*]

Dol. [*Pulls out handkerchief.*] Now don't you cry—if you do I'll throw up the case. [*She continues to sob.*] Didn't I tell you my news was both good and bad?

Hil. [*Looks up hopefully.*] Yes! Yes!

Dol. But I found that about the time you were married a leaf was torn out—and I'll stake my life that it was the record of your marriage.

Hil. But who could have done such a thing?

Dol. I strongly suspect that infernal villain of a husband of yours, to hide the evidence of your marriage to him!

Hil. Then I am lost! for he surely must have destroyed it. Oh, what shall I do—what shall I do!

Dol. Shut up! If you get me all excited, I'll have nothing to do with it. I don't believe he has destroyed it at all; but has it in his possession. I'm going to do a little detective work, and I warrant you that I'll spare no money to gain my point. I said I'd see this thing through, and hang me if I don't go my length in it.

Hil. Oh, thank you, sir!

Dol. Now listen to my plan. [*Noise heard, L. 2 E.*]

Hil. Some one approaches! Let us walk on a piece, where there is no danger of being overheard. [Exeunt HILDA *and* DOLLERCLUTCH, *R. 2 E.*]

Enter ANASTASIA, *L. 2 E., with letter in hand.*

Anas. [*Looks around.*] I have written a few lines to the dear man, just to encourage him a bit—he seemed so confused. I will leave it here on this bench. [*Lays it on bench R. C.*] He will surely come back and find it. George Washington Dollerclutch! Oh! he must be a brave man to

have such a grand name! [*Noise heard, R. 2 E.*] I hear
footsteps! It must be he returning—I'll retire for a few
moments. [**Exit** *L. 2 E.*]

Enter CORIOLANUS, *R. 2 E.*

Cor. How dare he lay violent hands upon me—a gentleman of nobility! I cannot suffer such indignity to pass unnoticed. [*Sees letter on bench.*] What's this! a letter?--
and her handwriting, too! [*Reads.*] "To one I love"--
hem! that's me! [*Opens it—reads.*] "Thou adorable one with the brave sounding name,"—she likes my name!
"Ever since our first meeting have you made the profoundest impression upon my heart."—I knew it! "Maidenly modesty has prevented me from making an open expression of my affection. My heart expands within my bosom. If you love me wear a red necktie and smile upon me when next we meet. With all maidenly reserve, I am yours, A. M." I will procure the necktie at once, and prepare to satisfy the longing of her heart with the knowledge that her love is returned. [**Exit** CORIOLANUS, *L. 2 E.*]

Enter HENRY, *gate C.*

Hen. [*With draft in hand.*] I think I have secured all the persons in the draft but two, and they are Coriolanus Wellington and George Washington Dollerclutch. That Dollerclutch has led me quite a chase—been looking for him two days. Wherever I've looked for him I was informed he had just left. I believe the rascal is dodging me. But I guess I'm sure of the other chap—he's a servant here with Adrienne's father-in-law. I'll go in and secure him. [**Exit** *into cottage.*]

Enter DOLLERCLUTCH *and* HILDA, *R. 2 E.*

Dol. Now you leave everything in my hands and I'll see that I bring you through your trouble all right. I've got all the points on this paper. Now go into the house before we are discovered. I'll soon bring the smiles back again.

Hil. Oh, thank you! Heaven bless you for befriending a helpless girl. [*Exit* HILDA *into cottage.*]

Enter ANASTASIA, *L. 2 E.* DOLLERCLUTCH *puts paper into pocket.*

Anas. [*Aside.*] He has just read my letter. Ahem!

Dol. [*Turns.*] My dear madam! Pray be seated! [*Leads her to bench R. C.*] I regret extremely that our last interview was so abruptly terminated by the advent of that ignorant jackass—

Enter CORIOLANUS, *L. 2 E., wearing a ridiculously large red necktie. He strikes dignified attitudes and tries to attract* ANASTASIA'S *attention to it. He tries to smile—but they are very sickly smiles.*

Anas. [*Stares at* CORIOLANUS.] Oh!

Dol. [*Aside.*] There's that confounded idiot again. Look at the grinning hyena.

Anas. Well, I never! The man must be crazy.

Dol. [*Rising.*] Madam! with your permission, I will crush the rascal. [ANASTASIA *nods assent.* DOLLERCLUTCH *bounces him—they struggle off L. 2 E. Sound of broken glass.* DOLLERCLUTCH *returns, his clothes ruffled.*] I guess I fixed him that time—I landed him in the hot-house.

Anas. [*Admiringly.*] I knew you were a brave man!

Dol. Well, I must say I am rather proud of my bravery. I was not named George Washington for nothing.

Enter HENRY *from cottage.*

Hen. [*Aside.*] At last! [*To* DOLLERCLUTCH.] George Washington Dollerclutch, I beg to inform you that you are drafted. You will accompany me to headquarters.

Dol. [*Terror-stricken.*] Oh, Lord!

Enter CORIOLANUS, *L. 2 E., face and hands cut—his clothes disordered.* ANASTASIA *R.*, DOLLERCLUTCH *R. C.*, HENRY *C.*, CORIOLANUS *L. C.*

Cor. What! I calmly submit to this outrage? Never! I'll tear him to pieces.

Hen. [*Seizing* CORIOLANUS.] You are drafted to help preserve the Union. [CORIOLANUS *is frightened. During the above* ANASTASIA *pantomimes to* DOLLERCLUTCH *to follow her and escape.* **Exit** ANASTASIA *R. 2 E.* DOLLERCLUTCH *about to follow her.* HENRY *sees him and points revolver at him.*] Halt! [DOLLERCLUTCH *turns and sees revolver and is frightened.*] Advance three paces—halt! About face! [CORIOLANUS *takes position on his right.*] That will do. Now, gentlemen, before we go to headquarters, you will accompany me into the house until I get some lunch; then we will proceed on our journey. Left face! Forward march! [**Exeunt** *all into cottage.*]

Enter ADRIENNE, *followed by* REGINALD, *L. 2 E.*

Reg. Adrienne!

Adri. [*R. C. Turns.*] Your pleasure, Reginald!

Reg. [*Quietly, but firmly.*] Adrienne, I desire a few moments' conversation. What I have to say is for your ears only!

Adri. Proceed, Reginald. I hear you!

Reg. Adrienne, the time has come when I must speak—I can no longer bear the cold, dignified reserve with which you treat me—your husband. There is a motive for all things—and there must be a motive that prompts your action. We are man and wife, and open candor and frankness should exist between us.

Adri. Have I not fulfilled my duty, sir? Have I not shown you the honor and respect that you have a right to demand from a wife?

Reg. You have honored and respected me, Adrienne, but I have a right to expect even more.

Adri. I do not understand!

Reg. I have a right to expect your love! [ADRIENNE *retreats a step, her hand pressed to her heart.*] Yes, Adrienne! Marriage is a holy act which ought to be based on the rock of love; else it becomes a sordid and disgraceful bargain, devoid of sacredness and heavenly sanction. [*She recoils.*] When I led you to the altar it was with the firm belief that our marriage would be a holy and sacred bond, founded upon the eternal principle of love. But your manner since has caused me to doubt the sincerity of your heart.

Adri. [*Haughtily.*] Did I, when I accepted your hand, say that I returned your love?

Reg. No! In my eyes you were an ideal woman, of the highest and noblest sentiment—devoid of worldly ambition and desire. That was sufficient. Could I then doubt the feeling which actuated your acceptance of my heart and hand? [*Slight pause.*] Adrienne! say that I am not disappointed in you—say that your sacred vow at the altar, "to love, honor and obey," was not a hollow sham—speak, Adrienne, speak! [*Pause.* REGINALD *turns away.*]

Adri. [*Recovering slowly.*] I will be honest with you, sir! You have a right to know. Could I but recall those fatal words that bound me for life to one I can never love, I would willingly lay down my life. I refused you when you first offered yourself, because I loved another. When I witnessed his perfidy, a few moments later, in a fit of pique, I accepted you. When I recovered from the mad impulse that swayed my being, I awakened to the misery into which I had plunged myself, and I almost hated you for tempting me to this agonizing bondage.

Reg. [*With intense feeling suppressed.*] Madam, the die is cast! You bear my name—you are my wife—that cannot be recalled, for that is recorded above. You will ever receive at my hands the respect that is due my wife. I shall provide for and protect you as long as He, in His good mercy, does grant me life. You will always find this, my paternal home, yours to enjoy.

Adri. [*Alarmed.*] What would you do?

Reg. Madam, it must be evident to you that my hopes in life are blighted; that I would not weary your sight with the presence of one who would be a constant reproach to your misery and folly. I will leave you. Perhaps the day may come when your heart may change and turn toward the husband. If so, the words, "Reginald, I love you—come back," will bring to your bosom the husband, who will always be true to his sacred vow at the altar. [*Crosses to L.*]

Enter HENRY, DOLLERCLUTCH *and* CORIOLANUS, *followed by* ANASTASIA, MORRIS *and* HILDA, *from cottage.* HENRY *back of bench, R.* DOLLERCLUTCH *and* ADOLPHUS, *R.* MORRIS *and* ANASTASIA, *up C.* HILDA *crosses to* ADRIENNE. ADRIENNE *is overcome. She sinks on bench, R. C.*

Reg. [*To* HENRY.] Henry, accept a new recruit, who is ready to fight for the preservation of the Union and protect the Stars and Stripes. [*Takes roll and pencil and signs it.*]

Adri. [*Starting up, with outstretched hands.*] Reginald, stay!

Hen. Too late! [ADRIENNE *faints.* HILDA *attends her at bench, R. C.*]

Tableau.

DOLLER.   CORIO.
HEN.   MORRIS.
HIL.   ADRI.   REG.   ANAS.

Curtain.

ACT III.

A Lapse of Four Years.

Scene 1: A Camp in the Army.

Discovered at rise of curtain: Henry *in Captain's uniform, and* Reginald *as a private, both seated on camp-stools, R. 2 E.* Coriolanus, *as private, sitting near the fire, R. C.* Dollerclutch, *as private, asleep in front of tent, L. 4 E.* Adolphus, *as private, doing sentinel duty, L. 1 E.*

Hen. When did you hear from home last, Reginald?

Reg. A week ago.

Hen. And how is your little Alice?

Reg. When last I heard, she was well. Oh, Henry! she is the only joy in my life. The future of my child is the only thing that keeps me from despair. I live in hopes that I shall one day clasp my child to my bosom. Oh, the yearning of a father's heart! And now that we are so near to her, I almost feel tempted to shirk my duty and satisfy the longing to see my beloved child.

Hen. We are only six miles away from your home, I believe you said?

Reg. Yes! day by day have we been drawing closer to it. And it is nearly four years since I left the scene, never to return to it again. [*He turns away.*]

Hen. Reginald, I sincerely sympathize with you in your trouble. [*Takes him by the hand.*] Adrienne has wronged you deeply. She——

Reg. [*Checks him.*] Henry, she is your sister, but do not forget that she is my *wife*. I cannot listen to her condemnation even from you.

Hen. Well, Reginald, I respect your wishes. But cheer up! I have faith to believe that all will be right again —that some day will see you reunited and happy.

Reg. [*Shakes his head.*] This will be my only happiness, Henry. [*Shows picture of child.*]

Hen. Is this the picture of my niece? Why, she doesn't look a bit like Adrienne!

Reg. No! the resemblance is to *my* family. I can now readily understand why my father wrote to me, soon after the child's birth, asking the privilege of naming it. She bears a striking resemblance to my little sister.

Hen. Your sister! I never knew you had a sister!

Reg. No! because that is the skeleton in our family closet. Her name was Alice. When but three months old she was stolen from the cradle. All effort to recover the child proved fruitless. Her disappearance has since remained a mystery. Grief over our loss brought my mother to an early grave. My father sacrificed his all in the hope of recovering the child, but all his efforts proved unavailing. This happened eighteen years ago, and we know not whether she be living or not, but we mourn her as dead.

Hen. And had you no suspicion as to who stole the child?

Reg. None. My father did not think he had an enemy in the world.

Hen. Strange! very strange! The ways of Providence are mysterious, and we must bow with resignation to His Divine Will. One moment, Reginald. [*To* ADOLPHUS.] Adolphus!

Adol. [*Salutes.*] Captain, I await your orders.

Hen. Go to the officers' tent and inquire whether the mail has arrived.

Adol. [*Salutes.*] All right, Captain! [**Exit** *L.* 1 *E.*]

Hen. [*To* CORIOLANUS.] Coriolanus! [CORIOLANUS *rises and salutes.*] Take his post as sentinel! [CORIOLANUS *salutes and takes his post.* *To* REGINALD.] It is remarkable what a change there is in Adolphus. When I drafted him I thought he would make a poor soldier, he was so cowardly; but he has turned out to be one of the bravest men in the regiment. A soldier's life has made a man of him.

Reg. It has, indeed! I have often wanted to ask you what ever became of his chum, Sammy. I thought you had drafted him, also.

Hen. I did; but he had plenty of money, and furnished a substitute. I wish the mail would arrive. [*Rises.*] By the way, Reginald, did your last letter mention anything about any of the rest of your household?

Reg. [*Rises.*] For instance, Hilda? Ha! ha! ha! Oh, you sly rogue! Henry, I remember a conversation we had, when you asked me to show you a woman devoid of fashion's frivolities—ha! ha! ha! Perhaps, now *you* can show one—ha! ha! ha! What! Henry, the recluse, the woman-hater, in love with a woman? Wonderful! Ha! ha! ha!

Hen. Well, I'll acknowledge the corn; but I didn't know a sensible woman until I met Hilda Wallace, whose quiet and unassuming manners struck the chord of affinity in my nature.

Reg. [*Takes him by the hand.*] Well, well, I'm glad of the transformation, and I hope your future will not be marred by disappointment. [DOLLERCLUTCH *snores.*]

Enter ADOLPHUS, *L.* 1 *E.*

Hen. [*To* ADOLPHUS.] Well?

Adol. [*Salutes.*] The mail has not arrived, Captain!
[REGINALD **Exits** *into tent, C.* DOLLERCLUTCH *snores.*]

Hen. Pshaw! just tickle that fellow with your boot!
[ADOLPHUS *about to do so.*]

Dol. [*Dreaming.*] Oh, Anastasia! [ADOLPHUS, *L. C.*
HENRY, *C.* DOLLERCLUTCH *asleep, L.* CORIOLANUS, *down
L.*]

Hen. Listen! He's dreaming!

Dol. Anastasia, beloved! oh, fly—fly to my arms!

Hen. Ha! ha! ha! I wonder whether she's got wings?
[DOLLERCLUTCH *talks again.*] But, listen!

Dol. [*Starting.*] The rebs are coming—the rebs are
coming! Where shall I hide myself? I'll be killed if I
stay here. [*Sits upright.*] Don't shoot! [*He fights im-
aginary rebels.*] Don't shoot—don't! [*Awakes.*]

Hen. Look out! the rebs are coming! Ha! ha! ha!

Dol. [*Getting on his feet. Aside.*] Confound it all! I
must have been dreaming.

Hen. Ha! ha! ha! We've found you out at last, old
Dollerclutch. You are a *brave* man, George Washington.
I thought I never did see you when we went into an
engagement—now I can account for it.

Dol. [*L. C.*] Sir! I have always been where the fight
was thickest.

Cor. [*Aside.*] After it was over.

Hen. *You* mean George Washington was—but I mean
George Washington Dollerclutch.

Dol. Sir! Do you mean to insinuate that my bravery
is a matter of doubt? You wrong me, sir! You wrong
me, I can assure you. My deeds of valor have saved the
day many a time—many a time. Do you understand? But
my modesty won't allow me to speak of them. Even in
my childhood was I noted for my bravery. I took Mrs.
Winslow's soothing syrup with the most unflinching cour-

age. Nothing would delight me more than a hand-to-hand encounter with a whole regiment of rebels. I would glory in the chance, sir! I have smelt powder many times. [*He shoots off his revolver, smells the smoke from the barrel, and struts the stage.* HENRY *whispers to* ADOLPHUS *and points to* DOLLERCLUTCH.]

Adol. [*Aside to* HENRY.] All right, captain; I understand! [*He steals off cautiously, L. 2 E.* HENRY *beckons to* CORIOLANUS *to follow him, enjoining caution.* **Exeunt,** *R. 2 E. All this is done unperceived by* DOLLERCLUTCH.]

Dol. To take me for a coward—bah! Gentlemen, you don't know! you—[*Turns and finds them gone.*] Hello! where the deuce did they go? [*Looks around in the different tents.*]

Enter ADOLPHUS, *L. 2 E., in a rebel suit, with gun and false whiskers. He is not noticed by* DOLLERCLUTCH. ADOLPHUS *brings his gun to shoulder and points it at* DOLLERCLUTCH.

Adol. [*L. C.*] Halt, and surrender. [DOLLERCLUTCH *at tent, R. 5 E. He turns suddenly in a fright—his knees knock together—he raises his hands and tries to speak.*] Don't move a muscle or I'll bore you.

Dol. [*C.*] Don't shoot! Oh, please don't shoot. Please, Mr. Rebel, I have sixteen small children. Oh! consider what will become of them when I am taken from them! [ADOLPHUS *drops his gun. Aside.*] Ah! that melted him! [ADOLPHUS *raises gun again.*] Oh! oh!

Adol. Remove your cap! [DOLLERCLUTCH *complies with all.*] Place it on the ground. Take off your coat. Place it with your cap! [ADOLPHUS *takes off his cap and throws it to him.*] Put it on! [*Takes off his coat and throws it to* DOLLERCLUTCH.] Put it on! [*He gathers up* DOLLERCLUTCH'S *clothes.*] Now sit down. [DOLLERCLUTCH *goes for* *stool.*] No, no, on the ground! Take hold of your toes! Now sit there till I come back. [**Exit** *L. 2 E.*]

Dol. [*Looking around.*] This is the toughest scrape I was ever in. The camp has been surprised by the rebels. They are all captured. Oh, Anastasia, I'm done for!

Enter HENRY, *R. 4 E., followed by* CORIOLANUS. ADOLPHUS *re-enters, L. 2 E., in his regular uniform.*

Hen. [CORIOLANUS *R.*, HENRY *R. C.*, DOLLERCLUTCH *C.*, ADOLPHUS *L. C. Pounces upon* DOLLERCLUTCH.] I've got the rebel, boys. Get some cords, quick! [ADOLPHUS *gets them, L. 3 E.*]

Dol. [*Struggling.*] Hold on, Captain! Let me go; it's me!

Corio. Let's hang the rebel to a tree, Captain! He's a spy!

Dol. I tell you, Captain, it's me—don't you hear me?

Adol. Let's tie him to a stake and riddle him with bullets.

Corio. [*Aside.*] I'll get even with him now for the indignity he heaped upon me four years ago.

Dol. [*Struggling.*] Oh!

Hen. I'll tell you what we'll do! We will give him a sound switching first. Then we'll hang him for a spy.

Corio. [*Eagerly.*] Let me do the switching, Captain. [*Gets switch, L. 3 E. Aside.*] I'll give it him hot!

Dol. Oh, Lord! I shall die! [CORIOLANUS *returns.*]

Corio. Now, you rebel, [*cuts him with switch*] how does that feel?

Dol. You infernal rascal! I'll—[CORIOLANUS *cuts him again.*] Oh!

Corio. Fits close, eh? [*Cuts again.*]

Dol. [*Struggling.*] Oh! oh! [*Pleads.*] Good Coriolanus, please—please don't! [CORIOLANUS *cuts again.*] Oh! Don't you know your old friend, Dollerclutch?

Corio. Dollerclutch? You? Oh, no! you're not Dollerclutch. Dollerclutch is a *brave* man. Oh, no! you're a black-hearted rebel. [*Cuts him again.*]

Dol. Oh! oh!

Hen. [*To* CORIOLANUS.] Hold! Let me look at him! Ha! ha! ha! It is Dollerclutch, by all that's wonderful! [*Releases* DOLLERCLUTCH.] Ha! ha! ha! a good joke!

Dol. [*Rises to his feet.*] A joke, sir? Do you call that a joke? But, I'll now give you an exhibition of my bravery, sir! [*Pounces suddenly upon* CORIOLANUS. *They struggle off, L.* 3 *E. All laugh.*]

Adol. I guess we've taken the conceit out of him, Captain!

Hen. Yes, I hope it will prove a wholesome lesson to him.

Enter RALPH, *L.* 2 *E., with letters, which he pulls from his pocket. A large wallet drops unnoticed by him from his pocket, near stool, L.* 2 *E.*

Ralph. [*C.*] Good afternoon, Henry!

Hen. [*Aside.*] The mail at last! [*To* RALPH.] Good afternoon, Murdell! The mail?

Ralph. [*R. C.*] Yes! [*Sorting letters.*] Any news from the front?

Hen. Yes! Grant has flanked Lee and is pressing him hard.

Ralph. Good! He'll worry him out soon. [*Hands letter to* HENRY.]

Re-enter DOLLERCLUTCH, *L.* 3 *E.*; CORIOLANUS, *L.* 2 *E.*

Hen. Thanks, Major! [*Retires up stage and reads letter.*]

Ralph. [*Reads from envelope.*] Adolphus Softhead!

Adol. [*Comes forward.*] Thank you, Major! [*Salutes, and retires up stage reading.*]

Ralph. [*As before.*] George Washington Dollerclutch.
Dol. [*Comes down.*] That's me, Major! [*He takes letter, salutes and sits on stool, near which pocket-book lies.*]

Enter REGINALD, *from tent.*

Reg. [*R. C., to* RALPH.] Anything for me, Major? [*Salutes.*]
Ralph. [*Coldly.*] Yes! [*Hands him letter.*]
Reg. Thank you, Major! [*Salutes and retires up stage reading.*]
Ralph. [*Looking after him.*] Curse him! How I hate him! The proud fool! Satisfied to remain a private! If he'd accepted promotion, as it was offered him from time to time, for his gallant bravery in the field, he would be my superior officer. As it is, he prefers to remain a private, because, as he says, his ambition does not aspire to receive the plaudits of his country. The commanding officers cannot find praise enough for his heroism in action. Curse him! [*To* HENRY *on right.*] Lowville, you will meet the officers in a half hour from now, for consultation.
Hen. All right, Major! [**Exit** RALPH, *L. 2 E.*]
Reg. [*Looking at letter.*] And yet no word from Adrienne! [**Exit** *into tent, R. 5 E.*]
Dol. [*At stool, L. 2 E., reads.*] "I long for the time when this cruel war is over, when I may receive my brave Dollerclutch to this maiden heart." Oh! this cruel war, to keep such fond hearts apart! Hello! Here is something on the other side—[*reads.*] "Hilda tells me to write you that she has not forgotten you, and God bless you!" No, nor have I forgotten her! Poor girl! I've watched him and pumped him, but I can't find out anything—he's as close as an oyster with—[*Sees wallet on ground.*] Hello! What's this? [*Picks it up.*] "R. M." Why, it's his! [*Looks around.*] H'm! I'll investigate! [*Opens it and*

pulls out papers. He unfolds one and jumps up excitedly.]
Hurrah! Hilda's marriage record, by the jumping jingo!
[*He looks around, places it in his pocket.*] Good! [*Unfolds another.*] H'm—'tis part of a letter—[*reads*] "of old Maitland"—something torn off and then—"of old Maitland"—[*reads further*] "Revenge is sweet. I can fancy how he grieves for his lost Alice!" [*Studies.*] Maitland! The devil! That's Reginald's name; but he says old Maitland—he's young; but he's got a father. Of course he has, and he's older than he. Certainly he is! How stupid I am! [*Studies again.*] H'm! [*Pulls out baby dress from his bosom and examines initials.*] A. M.! [*Jumps up.*] Eureka! by the jumping jingo! A.—Alice! M.—Maitland! That's Hilda's name, I'll stake my life! Here comes the rascal back. [DOLLERCLUTCH *puts letter in his pocket hastily—he leaves the wallet on the ground, where he found it—goes a little up stage and appears interested in his own letter.*]

Enter RALPH, *L. 2 E., as if hunting for something.*

Ralph. Confound it! I must have dropped it when I pulled those letters from my pocket! [*Sees wallet on ground.*] Ah! Here it is! safe! What a fortunate thing it did not fall into anybody's hands! Good! I'm a lucky dog! [**Exit** *L. 2 E.*]

Dol. [*Comes down and looks after him.*] Yes! and I'm a luckier dog. I can go you one better, my chap. George Washington, you did that slick—you're a trump! But how shall I get these papers to the poor girl? Confound it, I can't send them to her for fear they'll fall into his hands again. If I keep them he'll soon discover his loss and institute a search. If I hide them until the war is over, I might get shot by an infernal rebel, and then how will the poor girl know about them? Now, this *is* a dilemma!

[*Studies.*] I have it! It is only five or six miles to the place. I'll take them myself. I'll wait till dark, then I'll slip away. I can be back in three hours! [*Sudden thought.*] What if my absence should be discovered? Then I'll be in a pretty pickle! Court-martial—probably shot for a deserter. Ugh! [*Sudden determination.*] I'll risk it; I promised to see this thing through, and, hang it, George Washington Dollerclutch will stand by his word. Besides, I'll have a chance to see my charming Anastasia. That'll nerve me in the undertaking. [*Retires up stage and* **Exits** *into tent, L. 4 E. During the last speech the stage is gradually darkened.* HENRY *comes forward, C.*]

Hen. Dollerclutch! [DOLLERCLUTCH *sticks his head out of tent.*] You will serve as sentinel on the high rock for the night. Maitland, relieve Softhead. [*They salute and go to their respective posts.* DOLLERCLUTCH *on high rock, L.* 5 *E.* REGINALD, *L.* 1 *E.*] This is going to be a dark night. I'll turn in. [**Exit** HENRY, *L.* 2 *E. The rest retire to their tents.*]

Dol. Now for my journey! [*He comes down, gets a cloak from tent, L.* 4 *E., and steals away cautiously, R.* 3 *E.*]

Reg. [*L. C. In a study.*] "Adrienne has taught little Alice to pray for you." How strangely my father's words move me! Perhaps—but no! no!—that will never be! Adrienne must be forever dead to my yearning heart. When I entered the army I thought I had buried the joy of life forever. But love for my child has sprung from the ashes of my forlorn hopes, to cheer my drooping heart, like the oasis to the weary traveler of the desert. Oh! the longing of a father's heart! What would I not give to see her—speak to her. Oh! I feel as if I could not resist the temptation to go and have if but one look. Yes, yes—a soldier's life is uncertain—it may be the only opportunity to cast my eyes upon my darling Alice!

Enter RALPH, *L. 2 E.* *He pauses.* REGINALD *at C.*

Reg. I cannot resist the impulse. I must see my child! [**Exit** *hurriedly into tent, L. 5 E.* RALPH *watches him cautiously.*]

Re-enter REGINALD *from tent with cloak, and* **Exit** *hurriedly, R. 4 E.*

Ralph. What does this mean? Maitland leaving his post? He acts strangely, too! I'll follow him and see what he is up to. At last I have the opportunity to humble his pride in the sight of the commanding officers! [*He follows* REGINALD, *R. 4 E.*]

Quick Curtain.

ACT IV.

Scene 1 : Sitting-Room in the Maitland Cottage.

Anastasia *discovered seated knitting at table, L. C.*

Anas. War, and war, and war—and nothing but war! What earthly sense can there be in a lot of men standing up to be shot at, I'd like to know? Men making targets of themselves for others to practice shooting at! If they want to shoot so bad there are enough shooting galleries, where they can bang away to their hearts' content. But that's just the way with the men. They always will be doing things they ought not to. If the women only had the control of the Government, there would not be any war—never! Everything would be peace and harmony.

Enter Morris, *D. R. 3 E.*

Mor. [*R. C.*] Good morning, sister! Where is my little darling Alice?
Anas. Out in the garden with her mother and Hilda.
Mor. [*Anxiously.*] I am almost afraid to let them venture out of the house for fear there might be some rebels lurking in the neighborhood.
Anas. [*Drops knitting and rises.*] Good gracious, brother Morris! There is no danger of the fighting coming so close?
Mor. It is hard to tell how it will be. Warfare is very uncertain, although I do not think there is any immediate

danger. The rebels are fleeing towards the north-west, out of our track entirely. The Union forces are but six miles to our west.

Anas. What if they should turn back? What will become of us?

Mor. True; but I believe the greatest danger is past! The rebels have a determined pursuer, who will not be forced back. Grant is not the man to acknowledge defeat. He has entered the fight to win, and I have faith in him to believe that he will not turn his back upon the rebels until he has forced them to submission.

Anas. Just to think that we might all have been shot and cut up—ugh! It makes my blood run cold.

Mor. But the danger is not entirely over. The enemy is getting desperate. Their supplies are cut off, and I fear some depredation from foraging parties. I must caution them not to go out of sight of the house, and not to allow Alice out of hearing. It would tear my heart-strings should harm come to my darling little Alice.

Anas. Bless the sweet child! How she does grow. Ah! brother, she looks more and more like our poor lost Alice every day.

Mor. Anastasia! I beg of you do not re-open the old wound. Revive not the bitter memories of the past, which still have power to renew the agony of a father's woful loss. [*Turns away.*]

Anas. Forgive me, brother! I did not wish to make you feel sad. I'm too sympathetic—I'm—I'm— [*She sits and cries affectedly.*]

Mor. There, there! Don't let us have a scene. John is about ready to start for the post-office. If you have any letters to send, you will please have them ready. I will go and seek my little torment, Alice. [**Exit** *D. R. F.*]

Anas. [*Takes letter from pocket and reads it.*] Ah, how he loves the child! Should anything happen to Alice, it would kill him. [*Addresses letter.*] George Washington Dollerclutch, Esq. There, you brave man! I'm so afraid his lion courage will make him too venturesome. History will be full of his great deeds of bravery and valor. But I must hasten, or I shall be too late. [**Exit** *D. L. 2 E.*]

Enter HILDA, *D. R. 3 E. She goes to chair R. of table.*

Hil. How cruel is fate! The friend on whom I had based my hopes to help me sustain an honorable recognition before the world is debarred, by the cruel requirements of war, from clearing my name of the stain and reproach heaped upon it by a designing and depraved villain.

Enter ADRIENNE, *D. R. 3 E.*

Adri. What! brooding again, Hilda? Come, cheer up! Put a firm trust in the Almighty, and He will help you out of your great trouble.

Hil. I do! [*Rises.*] But, oh! it seems so long to wait!

Adri. Alas, yes! We are apt to question sometimes, if He has deserted us. But, rest assured, Hilda, He is all mercy and justice, and will, in His good time, bring the balm of peace and joy to the suffering heart.

Hil. Thanks, my lady! You have been so good to me.

Adri. Nay, Hilda! I deeply sympathize with you in your trouble, and I feel assured that your villainous husband will, some day, meet the punishment he so richly deserves.

Hil. Yes, my lady. How near he came to wrecking your happiness, also. It makes me shudder to think of it.

By Force of Impulse.

Adri. Yes, Hilda! but Heaven saved me from such a fate. It is with shame that I must acknowledge that I was so blinded to his real character as to love him. Thank Heaven, my eyes have been opened to his treachery and baseness.

Hil. Oh, my lady! I am so glad to know that you forgave my silence about his true character.

Adri. I could not blame you, Hilda. It was a bitter lesson, and I can only reproach my folly for listening to his ardent appeals of love. I thought him a gentleman of the highest honor, worthy of the love of a virtuous and innocent girl. But your exposure of his utter depravity has saved me from despair. It has awakened me to a keen sense of the great injustice I have done him who has honored me with his name—my husband. Oh, the agony I have inflicted upon that noble, trusting heart! Oh, that it was I that drove him from me by my wretched cruelty!—perhaps to meet his death upon the gory field of battle.

Enter MORRIS, *door in L. F. He pauses and listens.*

Adri. Oh, may the Heavenly Father spare his life and bring him safely back to this bleeding heart.

Hil. Oh, Adrienne! then you love him?

Adri. Love him, Hilda! Yea. I worship him. The grand nobility of his soul has inspired my heart with the strong, undying love of the wife.

Hil. And does Reginald know of the change of your heart?

Adri. Alas, no! Pride—foolish pride—has kept me from making the confession to him.

Hil. Adrienne, let me beseech you, then, to write to him at once, and bring the sunshine of joy to his wretched heart. Do not mar your own happiness by withholding the true state of your feelings. Think of your child—your darling Alice. Do not deprive her future of the happiness of a father's love.

Adri. I am so unworthy of him. Can he—will he forgive? [*Aside.*] His words when he left me—"Perhaps in time your feelings may change; if so, the words 'Reginald, I love you—come back,' will bring to your side one who will forever love you." [*To* HILDA.] Yes, yes, Hilda, you have taught me my duty. I will unburden to him my heart. I *will* say—" Reginald, I love you—come back." [MORRIS *comes forward. Down L.*]

Mor. God bless you, my daughter!

Adri. You here?

Mor. Forgive me, Adrienne, for being a listener. But I am glad, for it has convinced me how much I had wronged you in my thoughts. It has shown me the true and loving heart of a woman—of a true and loyal wife, who can yet be a pride to the loving heart of a husband, and a joy in the declining years of his father. I have treated you coldly, harshly, unjustly. I knew not the cause—the motive of your action. I looked but upon the result. I now ask, in all humility and deference, your forgiveness. [*He kneels to her.*]

Adri. Rise, most noble sir! I have naught to forgive! I, alone, am to blame. I have merited your censure by my conduct. Heaven grant it may not be too late to restore to your arms an honored and dutiful son, and to me a cherished and beloved husband.

Mor. [*Embraces her.*] Adrienne! [*Kisses her forehead.*] God bless you, my daughter! [*His head droops on her shoulder.* ADRIENNE *gives her hand to* HILDA, *who takes it in both her own. Picture. Whistle scene.*]

68   *By Force of Impulse.*

Scene 2: Wood Pass in 1st Groove. Night.

Enter Dollerclutch, *R. 1 E.*, *enveloped in cloak.*

Dol. I got safely away without being discovered. The camp was wrapped in slumber, not a soul stirring but the sentinels. [*Looks around.*] If I'm not mistaken, I must be near the house. Ah! some one approaches! [*He retires.*]

Enter Hilda, *L. 1 E.*

Hil. If Reginald could but return, how happy they would be! I left Adrienne writing to him, pouring out the love which will bring joy to his desolate heart. [*Sighs.*] And there's Henry, her brother! How my thoughts will always revert to him. So manly in his bearing—high in the appreciation of true worth. If I only were—but no! I must check the feeling that has sprung up here. [*Pressing her heart.*] I must not forget that my life is linked to another—

Dol. [*Aside.*] It's she! I'm sure it is!

Hil. [*Alarmed.*] What's that!—who's there? [Dollerclutch *comes forward.* Hilda *retreats, alarmed.*]

Dol. Don't be alarmed, my dear girl. Don't you know your old friend?

Hil. [*Comes forward doubtfully.*] Can it be possible? Mr. Dollerclutch?

Dol. Yes, my dear girl, your stanch friend, Dollerclutch. [*Takes her hand.*]

Hil. I'm so glad to meet you! But what brings you in this neighborhood? Perhaps you know— Oh, tell me, sir! Have you any news? Relieve my suspense, sir!

Dol. I have news, and good news—I've discovered all; now don't you faint. I've got the record of your marriage

—and I have found your parents. [HILDA *gets faint and staggers.*] Oh, Lord! I told you not to faint—what shall I do? [*He supports her.*]

Hil. [*Starting up.*] 'Tis over, sir! The sudden joy nearly overcame me.

Dol. Now take a strong grip of your nerves—now do—that's a good girl. I have not a minute to spare. I must get back to camp before my absence is discovered or I shall get myself in a tight place.

Hil. Pardon me, sir! I will be calm!

Dol. That's right! [*Takes papers from pocket.*] Now listen! I haven't the time to tell you how I was successful—that I'll do by letter—but I've got the proofs, and here they are. That is the record of your marriage, and this is part of a letter from which, I think, I have found out that you are the daughter of Morris Maitland.

Hil. [*Staggers.*] Mr. Maitland my father?

Dol. Now be careful, I tell you! Don't forget your nerves. Now listen to what I say. Take these papers and this dress to Morris Maitland. [*Hands her papers and baby dress.*] Tell him your story and I'll stake my life on it that he will find a daughter and you a father.

Hil. How can I ever repay you for your kindness to me? You have raised a burden from my life that was crushing me. Heaven bless you, sir! May you meet the reward that your large and magnanimous heart deserves.

Dol. I haven't got any such heart! you are mistaken—entirely mistaken. My action was in the line of duty—purely in duty, without any kindness whatever, do you understand? Now go! lose not a moment and be careful not to lose the papers. [*Gently forces her to L. 1 E.*]

Hil. I will, sir! and Heaven bless you. [**Exit** *L. 1 E.*]

Dol. Now, I've got that poor girl happy, now for my own happiness. If I could only meet my Anastasia! Now why the deuce didn't I ask that girl to tell her to come out a few moments? George Washington, you're an idiot to let a little excitement get away with your head. But who comes this way? [DOLLERCLUTCH *hides.*]

Enter RALPH, *R.* 1 *E.*

Ralph. So! Adrienne must be the magnet which drew him from his post of duty. I followed him like a ferret, and I'm sure that we are in the neighborhood of his home. Curse him, he can walk like a race horse! I had to run, at times, to keep up with him. Go to your Adrienne, you vain fool, go to the wife whose heart enshrines another. I wish you joy! But I too shall, perhaps, see an opportunity to speak to the proud and haughty beauty! If I do, I'll humble her pride--curse her! [**Exit** *L.* 1 *E.*]

Dol. [*Comes forward.*] Ralph Murdell, by the jumping jingo! What brings him to this neighborhood? No good, I'll be bound! If he should run across Hilda before she gets to the house it might upset all. No! not while old Dollerclutch can prevent it. I'll follow the rascal, and, if he as much as attempts to injure a hair of the girl's head, I'll treat his black carcass to an ounce of lead. Hang me if I don't see this thing through! [**Exit** *L.* 1 *E.* *Whistle scene.*]

Scene 3: SAME AS SCENE 1.

ADRIENNE *discovered at table, L. C., writing.* ALICE *in crib, L.* 4 *E.*

Adri. [*Sealing letter.*] 'Tis done at last! With what feelings of anxiety shall I count the hours until I have his reply! Will it bring happiness to my longing heart? Yes, yes! His is a love that time cannot change, nor separation dim! [*Goes to crib, L. 4 E.*] How sweetly she sleeps! [*She kneels in prayer.*] Heaven preserve my darling child! Watch over her with thy faithful love and guidance. Guard the father with thy holy protection from the dangers of this cruel war, and restore him safely to the bosom of his sorrowing family. [*Her head droops. After a slight pause she gets up hurriedly.*] I will take the letter to John, so that he will be sure to take it to the post-office the first thing in the morning. [**Exit** ADRIENNE, *D. L. 2 E.*]

After a pause **Enter** REGINALD, *D. R. F.; he looks around eagerly; places his gun against chair, R. 2 E.*

Reg. No one here? How my heart does beat in anticipation of seeing my beloved Alice. [*Looks around.*] Oh, the bitter memories that haunt my mind at the sight of each familiar object! [*Sees crib, L. 4 E. Goes to it eagerly and pulls curtain aside.*] My child! my Alice! Heavenly Father, I thank Thee! She sleeps. Oh, Thou being of innocence, free from the taint of a deceitful world, I will not disturb the peaceful quiet of thy innocent slumber. Let me feast my eyes upon my sleeping darling! [*He kneels.*] Let the sweet picture of purity and innocence be forever hung in the desolate cavern of my bleeding heart, safely to guide me to that eternal home where the soul can find a haven of peace and rest! [*His head sinks.*]

Enter ADRIENNE, *door L. 2 E. She goes to R. C. and sees* REGINALD. *She is alarmed.*

Adri. What means this? A stranger!

Reg. [*Rises suddenly and turns.*] Adrienne! [*He turns away.*]

Adri. Reginald! [*She pauses, with heaving bosom.*]

Reg. I beg your pardon, Adrienne, for this intrusion. The impulse to see my child caused me to forsake my post of duty. It led me here to have but one look upon her darling form. I have been satisfied and I am ready to return to the stern post of duty. [*He turns to go towards door in L. F.*]

Adri. And have you no word for me? [*He pauses.*] Not a look for the mother of your child? [REGINALD *keeps his back towards her.* ADRIENNE *stretches her arms towards him.*] Am I so soon forgotten? [*He presses his brow. Pause.*] Reginald, I love you! come back! [REGINALD *turns suddenly and springs towards her.*]

Reg. Adrienne! [*She falls into his arms.*] My beloved Adrienne!

Adri. [*After a pause.*] Now am I happy, indeed! My prayers have been answered!

Reg. Heaven is, indeed, merciful, in bringing this joy into my dreary existence! I fulfilled my duty as a soldier more with the desire to die in the service of my country, than to live. But now, I enter the fight doubly armed, for I now know that I have something more to live for besides my child—a loving wife.

Adri. Heaven grant you will be spared to us, Reginald!

Reg. We will put our trust in Him above, who has granted me the boon of this happy hour! Alas that I must tear myself away from my new found joy! But duty demands that I return at once to my post.

Adri. Nay, Reginald, I cannot let you go again.

Reg. Alas! Adrienne, you must bear the separation calmly, for my sake and for the child's. I left my post without permission, and should my absence be discovered I shall be court-martialed. A few hours ago I feared not the consequences of my rash act. But now I dread it, for your sake. I must return at once, while there is yet time. Let the thoughts of our child be your strength in my absence, as she will be mine in the heat of battle. May the

Lord of Hosts bring this bloody war to a speedy close. [*Goes to crib.*] Farewell! my child! [*Kisses her.*] Farewell! my beloved wife! [*Kisses her. She clings to him.*] Heaven guard and keep you. [REGINALD *tears himself from* ADRIENNE *and* **Exits** *door L. F. hurriedly, leaving his gun behind.* ADRIENNE *sinks into chair R. of table.*]

Adri. Cruel, cruel fate! [*Her head droops.*]

Enter RALPH, *door R. F.*

Adri. [*Starts up joyfully.*] Reginald! [*Sees it is* RALPH. *She draws herself haughtily erect.*] Ralph Murdell!

Ralph. [*Comes down R. Sneeringly.*] Even I, Adrienne, your humble servant!

Adri. What means this intrusion, sir, at this hour of the night?

Ralph. I never had the pleasure of congratulating you before on your happy marriage!

Adri. Sir, you will oblige me by leaving this house!

Ralph. [*Aside.*] That cut, did it? [*To* ADRIENNE.] Pardon me, madam, but if you will allow me to offer my sincere sympathy for your loveless married life——

Adri. Leave this house instantly, or I will call assistance to eject you forcibly!

Ralph. Ha! ha! ha! I made sure there was no one about to disturb us ere I entered.

Adri. What do you mean?

Ralph. Just this! That there is not a soul within the reach of your voice. We are alone. But listen to me, Adrienne. I do not wish you harm—on the contrary, I offer you happiness.

Adri. I do not understand you, sir!

Ralph. When you married Reginald Maitland, it was not because you loved him, but to gratify a feeling of pique. You gave him your hand, but not your heart. That belonged to me! I have watched your husband every day and have read the unhappiness and misery that he tries to conceal. Adrienne, you are unhappy in the bonds that tie you to a loveless life. Therefore, fly with me, and I will show you a life's loving devotion — a life——

Adri. Enough! Do not pollute further the sanctity of a true and honest husband's roof with the vile utterances of depraved villainy. My husband I adore, and I will be loyal to him and faithful unto death. Your influence over my heart is forever broken, and I would sooner suffer death, aye, a thousand times, than to listen to another word from you, whom I hate and despise—yea, whom I loathe more than a viper in my path! Go, and may Heaven have mercy on your soul! [*She turns away in majestic contempt.*]

Ralph. [*Sees* REGINALD's *gun and takes it.*] Curse you! Those words have sealed your doom! [*He shoots.* ADRIENNE *staggers and falls.*] Ha! ha! ha! Now, my proud beauty, perhaps your pride is humbled! Ha! ha! ha! [*Looks around cautiously, puts out light, then gropes for door.*]

Enter DOLLERCLUTCH, *door R. F.*

Dol. [*Feeling in the dark.*] I'm sure he came this way—and that shot! I'm afraid all is not right. [*Runs into* RALPH.] Ha! [*They struggle.* RALPH *throws* DOLLERCLUTCH *from him and escapes through door, R. F.*] Confound it! He's got away! But I've got his ring, which slipped from his finger into my hand. He shan't escape—I'll have him yet. [**Exit** *hurriedly, door R. F.*]

By Force of Impulse.

After a pause **Enter** REGINALD, *door L. F.*

Reg. The house is dark. Adrienne has retired for the night. In the excitement and haste of my departure I forgot my gun. [*He feels around in the dark.*] I stood it here against a chair! [*Finds it.*] Ah! It would not do to return without it. I feel almost tempted to call Adrienne, that I might once more clasp her to my heart—but, no! I have delayed too long already. I will live on the fond remembrance of our happy meeting, and pray that the day be not far distant when I can feast my heart upon the smiles of my beloved wife and child! [**Exit** *door R. F.*]

Quick Curtain.

ACT V.

Scene 1: Camp; Same as Third Act.

Table, R. 2 E. Coriolanus *on duty as sentinel, L. 1 E.* Adolphus *in front of tent, C., cleaning gun;* Colonel Morrell, Captain Lowville *and* Major Murdell *at table, R. 2 E., in consultation, as curtain rises.*

Colonel Morrell. I agree with you, gentlemen, fully, and I have concluded not to advance further until I receive more definite news of the movements of the main body. We will, therefore, continue in camp till I give you further instructions.

Hen. According to all reports, the rebs are badly crippled, and Lee cannot hold out much longer. At all events, I should not be surprised to hear of his surrender to Grant in the near future.

Mor. Yes, there is all prospect of a speedy ending of this bloody strife, and I hope we will soon have peace restored, that we may be enabled to return to our homes and families! [*About to rise.*]

Ralph. One moment, Colonel! before you go! It is with regret that I must call your attention to a private in our command who deserted his post as sentinel!

Mor. Indeed! His name!

Ralph. Reginald Maitland! [Henry *rises.*]

Mor. [*Jumps up.*] What! Reginald Maitland? Impossible!

Ralph. [*Rises.*] I beg your pardon, Colonel, but it is a fact!

Hen. Surely, Major, you must be mistaken !

Mor. Reginald Maitland—a soldier ever ready to respond to the call of duty; always fulfilling his orders in the most praiseworthy manner — he desert his post? [*Shakes his head.*] Please explain, Major!

Ralph. 'Tis surprising, indeed! but, nevertheless, a fact! I saw him leave myself—he seemed to be greatly agitated. He was absent three hours!

Mor. Enough! Send for him to report to me at once!

Ralph. [*To* ADOLPHUS.] Adolphus! [ADOLPHUS *salutes.*] Request Private Maitland to report to Colonel Morrell immediately! [ADOLPHUS *salutes and goes to tent, R.* 5 *E.*]

Hen. [*Aside.*] Strange! What can it mean?

Ralph. [*Aside.*] At last!

Enter REGINALD *from tent; he comes down and salutes.*
RALPH, *R.*, HENRY, *R. C.*, COL. MORRELL, *C.*, REGINALD, *L. C.*, ADOLPHUS, *L.*

Reg. Colonel Morrell, I'm at your service, sir!

Mor. Maitland, were you not detailed as sentinel last night?

Reg. I was, sir!

Mor. Did you fulfill your duty to the letter? [REGINALD *hangs his head.*] You are silent! Speak!

Reg. Colonel Morrell, it is with shame I acknowledge that I have proved unfaithful to my duty—I deserted my post, sir!

Mor. Maitland, it pains me to know that you, on whose honor and probity I would have staked my existence, should be guilty of this offense. It is with regret that I am obliged to perform the duty which devolves upon me!

Reg. Colonel, the offense is a grave one. I have merited the punishment it demands. I am ready to receive it.

Mor. What was your motive in forsaking duty?

Reg. It was an uncontrollable impulse to see my child, whom I had never seen before, that swayed my being—I knew not what I did! My heart was filled with a mad desire to see my child. Duty, honor, all was forgotten. I could not resist the longing, the yearning of the father, but I followed the impulse which completely overpowered my reason.

Mor. And do you know that the penalty for your offense, according to the rules and regulations of war, is death?

Reg. I do! and I will not shrink from receiving my punishment. I am ready, Colonel, to receive sentence.

Hen. [*Aside.*] As fearless and brave as a lion!

Mor. [*Aside.*] No! I cannot do it! [*To* REGINALD.] Maitland, under the circumstances, and in consideration of your past praiseworthy service, and your undaunted gallantry in action, I will not execute the punishment which the offense merits.

Hen. [*Aside.*] Bravo, Colonel!

Ralph. [*Aside.*] Curse his sympathy!

Mor. But I cannot let the matter pass unnoticed. I place you under arrest for three weeks. You will be confined in the guard-house under close surveillance. Private Softhead, deprive him of his arms and accoutrements, and conduct him in disgrace to the guard-house. [ADOLPHUS *takes* REGINALD'S *gun, etc., and places them on the table.*]

Ralph. [*Aside.*] How it cuts his proud nature!

Hen. [*Aside to* MORRELL.] These are hard lines, Colonel!

Mor. [*Aside to* HENRY.] Yes, Captain! I regret it sincerely! I never before was obliged to do anything that gave me so much pain. But duty, as a true soldier, demanded it!

Adol. [*To* REGINALD.] Right face! Forward march. [**Exit** REGINALD *and* ADOLPHUS, *R. 4 E.*]

Cor. [*Looking off L. 2 E.*] Halt! Who goes there? [*Voice off entrance,* "Friend bearing dispatches for the commanding officer."] Advance, and deliver! [CORIOLANUS *gets them and hands them to* COLONEL MORRELL.] Colonel, allow me! [*He salutes and retires to his post.*]

Mor. [*Opening dispatches.*] What's this? Can I believe my eyes? [*Reads.*] "Adrienne Maitland, the wife of Reginald Maitland, was found last night, shot in the head. From the evidence I have collected, I am satisfied that the husband is the murderer. I send you the proofs. H. Carson, Chief of Police." No! no! I cannot believe that that man is guilty of such an infamous charge. [*To* RALPH.] Major! read that, and say if that is not the most outrageous lie against such an honorable soldier as Reginald Maitland! [*Hands him paper.*]

Ralph. [*Aside.*] Ha! ha! ha! Now will I have my revenge.

Hen. How now, gentlemen, have you bad news?

Mor. There! [*Pointing to paper.*] Read for yourself! [RALPH *hands* HENRY *paper.*]

Hen. Merciful father! Adrienne killed! [*Staggers.*] My sister shot? [*With force.*] Tell me, Colonel, who is the cowardly wretch that committed this deed? [RALPH *shrugs his shoulders.*]

Mor. [*Pointing to paper in* HENRY's *hand.*] Read!

Hen. [*Looks on paper.*] No! no! no! What! he guilty of her murder! No! a thousand times no! I would just as readily believe an angel guilty of the crime as I would Reginald Maitland! No! I will wager my life on his innocence!

Ralph. [*Sneeringly.*] But everybody is not likely to share your opinion!

Mor. [*Taking* HENRY *by the hand.*] Lowville, I agree

with you! I cannot believe so noble a character invested with so foul a heart! Let us investigate the proofs! [*He unfolds another paper. Reads.*] "I inclose the deposition of William Harding, who swears that he saw Reginald Maitland prowling about the premises in a cautious and suspicious manner, and that he saw him enter the house about half past nine o'clock, which was about the time when the deed was committed."

Hen. That evidence proves nothing, Colonel.

Ralph. It is very significant though!

Mor. One moment, gentlemen! [*Reads.*] "I also inclose a piece of blackened paper, evidently the wadding of the gun—also a bullet which we found imbedded in the wall." [*He pulls blackened paper from envelope—he smells it.*] The wadding of the gun! [*He smooths it out.*] There is writing upon it! H'm! part of a letter. [*Reads.*] "i-l-d Alice!" i-l-d? child Alice, that's it! "loving fath—" father, I suppose—" Morris Mai—" the rest is burned away.

Ralph. A letter from his father. [*To* HENRY.] The evidence is getting strong, Captain, is it not? [HENRY *is silent.*]

Mor. [*Takes bullet from envelope.*] The fatal bullet! [*Examines it.*] Here are two letters on it, R. M.

Ralph. Gentlemen, the evidence is conclusive—he is guilty.

Mor. Do not be hasty, Major! I am not yet satisfied of his guilt. [*Aside.*] I fear the worst. [*To* ADOLPHUS.] Adolphus! conduct Private Maitland here at once! [ADOLPHUS *salutes and* **Exits** *R. 4 E.*]

Ralph. [*Aside.*] He cannot escape now.

Hen. [*Aside.*] Alas! I fear the result!

Enter REGINALD *and* ADOLPHUS, *R. 4 E.*

Mor. Maitland, I have evidence here which accuses you of murder!

Reg. [*Recoiling.*] Murder? I, Colonel? I accused of murder?

Mor. Yes, you!

Reg. [*Quietly.*] Whom am I accused of murdering?

Mor. Your wife!

Reg. [*Staggers.*] My wife?—my wife? my Adrienne murdered?—merciful father! [*Pause. With forced calmness.*] I beg your pardon, Colonel, but I pray you make me not a victim of such cruel jest! [MORRELL *turns away.*] No! no! Tell me 'tis but a jest—tell me it is not true. Oh, Colonel, tell me that my Adrienne lives—lives—lives! [*He is silent. To* HENRY.] Henry, end this suspense, this torture. Is Adrienne dead?

Hen. [*Taking his hand.*] Yes, Reginald, it is true!

Reg. Alas!—alas! [*His head droops. Slight pause. With force.*] Who—who is the hellish fiend that robbed me of my Adrienne? Tell me, that I might tear his cowardly body limb from limb.

Mor. Maitland, you alone are accused of the crime. [*To* ADOLPHUS.] Softhead! you will take down in writing the proceedings of this examination. [ADOLPHUS *at table R.,* HENRY, *R. C.,* RALPH *near table,* COL. MORRELL, *C.,* REGINALD, *L. C.,* CORIOLANUS, *R. To* REGINALD.] Are you guilty or are you not guilty of the murder of your wife, Adrienne Maitland?

Reg. I murder Adrienne—my wife? ha! ha! ha!—no! She, in whose happiness my whole soul was wrapped up? No—no

Mor. Answer, guilty or not guilty!

Reg. Not guilty!

Mor. [*To* RALPH.] At what hour did he desert his post?

Ralph. Eight o'clock!

Mor. [*To* REGINALD.] At what hour were you in company with your wife?

Reg. About nine o'clock!
Mor. Did you have your gun with you?
Reg. I did!
Mor. When did you load it last, and where?
Reg. Yesterday morning, in my tent!
Mor. Did you discharge it since?
Reg. No, sir!
Mor. Is it still loaded?
Reg. It is, sir!
Mor. Major Murdell, hand me Maitland's gun. [*He examines it.*] Gentlemen, the gun has been discharged! [*He hands gun back—he then hands* REGINALD *blackened paper.*] Do you recognize that paper?
Reg. [*Looks at paper.*] I do! It is part of a letter from my father! I used it for wadding.
Mor. Do you recognize this bullet? [*Hands it.*]
Reg. [*Examines.*] It is from my mould.
Mor. Did you have any ill feeling against your wife?
Reg. None!
Ralph. Colonel, I can prove that there has existed bad feeling between them since their marriage!
Mor. Make your statement!
Ralph. They lived unhappily together until an open rupture caused him to leave her and enlist in the army.
Mor. Your proof! [RALPH *points to* HENRY.] Lowville, do you corroborate Major Murdell's assertion? [HENRY *looks at* REGINALD. HENRY *is silent.*]
Reg. Speak, Henry!
Hen. [*Aside.*] Must I speak? [*After a pause, to* MORRELL.] I do!
Mor. [*To* REGINALD.] What was the nature of the rupture?
Reg. I decline to answer.
Ralph. That was his motive for the crime!

By Force of Impulse. 83

Mor. Silence! [*To* REGINALD.] In the face of the evidence, I am forced to believe you guilty. I regret that a soldier such as you have heretofore proved yourself to be, should come to such an ignominious end. [RALPH *consulting with others.* HENRY *walks aside.*]

Reg. Do you believe me guilty, Colonel? [*He turns from* REGINALD.] And do you all think me guilty of this cowardly crime? [*They all look away but* HENRY, *who takes* REGINALD *by the hand.*]

Hen. No! I would believe you innocent, had they ten times the evidence.

Ralph. The evidence has proven his guilt most conclusively!

Mor. [*To* REGINALD.] Have you anything to say why I should not pass sentence upon you?

Reg. I have not!

Hen. Oh, Reginald, why do you not defend yourself? Why not make an effort to prove your innocence?

Reg. Henry, what have I to live for now? Adrienne is gone from me. She has left the world dark and dreary to me. I long to join her there! [*Points upward.*]

Hen. Prove your innocence. Let not the stain of murder rest on your honorable name!

Reg. Henry, this is but the judgment of men. I bow to the judgment of Him alone who knoweth all things. He knows I am innocent—that is sufficient. I am satisfied! His will be done! [*To* MORRELL.] Colonel, I await your orders!

Mor. [*Aside.*] I would I could believe him innocent. The evidence condemns him! [*Sighs.*] I must fulfill my duty! [*To* REGINALD.] Maitland, the evidence that has been brought to bear shows conclusively that you are guilty! Nothing remains but for me to pass sentence. I therefore condemn you to be shot until you are dead.

[REGINALD *bows his head.*] The sentence shall be executed immediately. I will allow you five minutes to prepare yourself to meet your God! [*Takes out watch. To* RALPH.] Major! you will detail your men to execute the order. [RALPH *whispers to* CORIOLANUS *and* ADOLPHUS.]

Hen. [*To* REGINALD.] Reginald, this is terrible! The Colonel has no right to use such haste. The evidence is purely circumstantial, and should require deeper investigation!

Reg. Nay, do not blame Colonel Morrell; he has simply done his duty. Besides, why should the execution be deferred? Why should I longer drag out a miserable existence? I will soon be happy, Henry, for I shall meet Adrienne. But my child, Henry! my darling little Alice! Take her, Henry—be a father to her—guide her footsteps in the path of honor and virtue. Teach her not to despise her father—that he is innocent. Teach her not to listen to the sneers of the world, but to place an everlasting faith in the Father of us all, so that at the last she will find peace and joy in the beautiful realms above!

Hen. I accept the trust, Reginald. God grant I will be faithful to it. [*They shake hands.*] Have you any further wishes?

Reg. Tell my father I am innocent—that will be sufficient—he will believe me. Now leave me, Henry!

Hen. Farewell, my brother! [*They embrace.*] Farewell! [REGINALD *kneels a moment with bowed head in silent prayer, after which he rises with a quiet air.*]

Reg. I am ready, Colonel! [MORRELL *waves his hand.* ADOLPHUS *blindfolds* REGINALD, *ties his hands behind him, and places him in position, L. C.* ADOLPHUS *and* CORIOLANUS *take position on right.*]

Ralph. [COLONEL MORRELL, *R.,* HENRY, *R. C.,* RALPH, *R. C.,* CORIOLANUS *and* ADOLPHUS *up R.,* REGINALD, *L. C. Pulls* *handkerchief from pocket.*] Carry arms! Ready! [*Holds handkerchief at arm's length.*]

Enter DOLLERCLUTCH, *R. 4 E.*, *hurriedly.*

Dol. [*C.*] Hold! If you shoot that man you commit murder! He is innocent!

Mor. [*R. C.*] What mean you?

Ralph. Will you allow this interference, Colonel?

Mor. Yes! God forbid that I should shoot an innocent man! [*To* DOLLERCLUTCH.] Your proofs!

Dol. My proofs are crushing! There is no murder! [REGINALD *pulls off handkerchief.*] His wife lives. She is even now on her way to this camp!

Reg. Adrienne lives? Thanks be to God!

Mor. How do you know this?

Dol. I overtook her on the road on my way to camp. She was almost exhausted, and begged of me to run on and save Reginald from being shot for her murder. I did so, and here I am, just in the nick of time! By jingo, I feel so good, I could shake hands with the greatest scoundrel that ever breathed. [*He shakes* RALPH's *hand.*]

Ralph. Colonel, you surely will not be imposed upon by that rascal's concocted story?

Mor. Silence! If she is not dead, it was not the fault of the intended murderer. He meant to kill her, and the intent is sufficient for which to carry out the penalty!

Dol. [*R. C.*] Correct, Colonel! But that man is not the one who attempted the murder. I swear that Reginald Maitland left the house fifteen minutes before the shot was fired. I was watching one whom I know to be the murderer, prowling around the house; but looking after Maitland's departure, I lost sight of the other chap. Some time after I heard the shot and rushed into the house and into the arms of the attempted assassin, who was trying to escape. I struggled to overpower him, but he was too much for me. [*Rubs his side and grimaces.*] He got away. I pursued, but he got off in the darkness. In my eagerness to catch him, I fell into the hands of the rebels.

Mor. And how did you get away from the rebels?

Dol. This morning, by indomitable bravery and courage, I fought my way out of their lines and hastened back here to camp.

Mor. Who is the man that attempted the deed?

Dol. The room was dark; the scoundrel had put out the light; I could not recognize him!

Ralph. [*Aside.*] Safe! safe!

Mor. How do you know, then, that it was not Maitland?

Dol. In the struggle, the villain's ring slipped into my hand. Here it is, Colonel! [MORRELL *takes and examines it.*] Later I also found this shoulder strap hanging to one of my buttons. [MORRELL *hands ring to* RALPH.] Colonel, do privates wear these things?

Ralph. Colonel, here are some letters engraved on the seal—R. M. Reginald Maitland!

Dol. You lie! R. M.—Ralph Murdell, and here is where this belongs, you cowardly assassin! [*He claps the shoulder strap on* RALPH's *shoulder, which is minus one.*]

Mor. Men, secure him! [ADOLPHUS *and* CORIOLANUS *do so.* HENRY, *R.,* CORIOLANUS, RALPH *and* ADOLPHUS, *R. C.,* COLONEL MORRELL, *C.,* DOLLERCLUTCH *and* REGINALD, *L. C.*]

Ralph. [*To* DOLLERCLUTCH.] Curse you for a meddlesome hound!

Dol. I said I would, and so I did, by jingo!

Enter ADRIENNE, *R. 4 E., out of breath; her head is bandaged; she is very pale and exhausted.* REGINALD *takes C.*

Adri. Reginald, my husband!

Reg. Adrienne! [*She falls in his arms half fainting.*]
Adri. Safe! safe! You are safe!
Reg. Yes, yes, my wife. Heaven is just! You have been spared to me by His great mercy.
Mor. [*Approaching them.*] Pardon me, Maitland, for interrupting. Allow me to ask you one question, Madam? [*She nods.*] Who was it that fired the shot?
Adri. [*Pointing to* RALPH.] There stands the coward who, failing in his effort to make me unfaithful to my true and loyal husband, attempted to murder me!
Mor. [*To* REGINALD, *taking his hand.*] Forgive me, Maitland, for entertaining one moment the thought that you were guilty of such cowardly villainy! I have wronged you deeply.
Reg. I have naught to forgive, Colonel; you have acted only as a true soldier, and, had you not done as you did, you would have neglected your duty.

Enter HILDA, *R.* 4 *E.*

Hil. [*L. C., to* ADRIENNE.] You are safe, Adrienne. You rushed from the house in your frantic excitement. I feared your mind was wandering.
Adri. Nay, Hilda! When I learned that my husband was accused of my supposed murder, I dreaded the consequences, and determined to save him ere it was too late.
Hil. They knew not where you had fled. But I knew where your heart would lead you, and I followed.
Hen. [*Aside.*] What a wealth of true womanly feeling is hidden by her quiet demeanor! [*To* HILDA.] Will you be kind enough to enlighten us, how it was that we received news from the Chief of Police that Adrienne was murdered?

Hil. When we found her last night, we supposed her to be dead, until this morning I thought I detected signs of life. I begged of them to summon a physician at once. He pronounced her alive, but in a death-like stupor. After hard work she was restored to consciousness. Examination of her wound showed that the bullet had only grazed the head, inflicting a scalp wound, but sufficient to effectually stun her.

Hen. Kind Providence turned the bullet's fatal course, but it was almost the means of bringing a noble life to an ignominious end. [*Pointing to* REGINALD.]

Hil. Have you discovered the real culprit?

Hen. Yes! he is there! [*Points to* RALPH.]

Hil. [*Staggers.*] Ralph!—my husband?

Hen. Your husband? Is that man your husband?

Hil. Alas! yes! With what feelings of loathing must I make the acknowledgment.

Ralph. Bah! you she-devil! I never married you—you were only a mistress!

Dol. You lie, you black-hearted villain!

Hil. [*Producing papers.*] You could ruin my character in the eyes of the world did I not possess this! [*Holding paper aloft.*] The record of my marriage to you. [RALPH *recoils.*]

Dol. [*To* RALPH.] And I was the individual who saved that girl from your base villainy! I—do you understand?—I!

Ralph. Curse you!

Hen. [*Aside.*] Alas for my hopes!

Enter MORRIS *and* ANASTASIA, R. 4 E.

Anas. [*Going to* ADRIENNE *and embracing her.*] You dear child! How glad I am that we've found you at last!

Mor. Heaven be praised, my daughter, I find you safe. [*He embraces* REGINALD.] My son!

Reg. Father!

Mor. I am overjoyed at this happy union of loving hearts. [*To* HILDA.] Alice, my child! [*Beckons her to come. To* REGINALD.] Reginald, God has been merciful to restore to us your lost sister—my darling daughter, Alice!

Reg. My sister?

All. Your daughter?

Mor. Yes! my daughter! [*Embraces her.*] After many years of suffering and anguish has Heaven sent me the joy that I thought was buried in the past. [*Takes* DOLLERCLUTCH *by the hand.*] Here is the instrument of Providence who saved an innocent girl and brought happiness to a father's heart. [HILDA *converses with* HENRY.] Bless your kind heart! How can I ever repay you?

Dol. Tut! tut! tut! I acted only on business—only on business, sir!—do you understand? Entirely on business —without any kindness whatever. I am more than repaid when I see the happiness and joy that surrounds me! [*He goes to* ANASTASIA. *Up L. C.*]

Mor. That man's father [*pointing to* RALPH] was the wretch who stole the child from our parental bosom! His father and I aspired for the hand of the same lady—I was the successful one. He, being of a very passionate and revengeful nature, darkened our domestic bliss by stealing from the cradle our youngest child, Alice! I did not think I had an enemy in the world who could be guilty of such baseness, until last night I received the proof which exposed him and restored to me a daughter. All doubts of her identity were removed by the discovery of a mole behind her left ear, which we remembered our child's having.

Morrell. I congratulate you, sir, upon your new found joy! The mills of justice grind slowly sometimes, but they are sure. Righteousness and truth will always receive its blessed reward. [*To* CORIOLANUS *and* ADOLPHUS.] Men, remove the depraved scoundrel to the guard house and see that he is strongly guarded. [*They do so.* **Exit** RALPH, CORIOLANUS *and* ADOLPHUS, *R. 2 E.*] It is a pity to mar the happiness of this hour with the presence of such a vile and cowardly rascal! [*To* REGINALD.] Maitland, in consideration of the terrible mistake and injustice by which I almost sacrificed your life, I hereby revoke the order for your disgrace and restore you to honorable recognition by promoting you to the position of Major!

Hen. Bravo, Colonel!

Dol. Good! your heart is in the right place, Colonel! [*Aside.*] And so is mine! [*Turning to* ANASTASIA.]

Reg. [*Taking* MORRELL *by the hand.*] Thanks, Colonel, thanks!

Morrell. Do not thank me, Maitland; you are more than deserving. Had you accepted promotion before when it was offered, for your gallant conduct and bravery on the field, you would long since have been even my superior officer. [*A shot is heard.*] What's that? [*All are alarmed and look off entrance.*]

Enter ADOLPHUS *and* CORIOLANUS, *R. 2 E.*

Adol. [*R.*] He's done it, Colonel!—he's done it!

Morrell. Done what? Who?

Adol. Ralph Murdell! He pulled a revolver and shot himself through the head.

Cor. Yes! His rash act has precipitated him into eternity—he's dead!

Morrell. [*Shrugs his shoulders.*] Well, he has only saved me the stern duty of condemning him to such a fate.

Hen. [*Aside.*] His act has freed Hilda from the yoke of misery and despair. [*Commotion outside. Voices heard crying* "Hurrah!" *in the distance.*]

Morrell. What means this excitement? Dollerclutch, go and learn the cause! [**Exit** DOLLERCLUTCH, *L. 2 E., hastily.*] They are yelling hurrah! There must be some good news from the front. They seem wild with joy!

Re-enter DOLLERCLUTCH, *L. 2 E.*

Dol. [*Rushing around excitedly.*] Hurrah! hurrah! hurrah!

Morrell. [*Stopping him.*] Give us the news.

Dol. Hurrah! The war is over! Lee has surrendered to Grant!

Omnes. Hurrah! hurrah! hurrah! [*Wild excitement and joy.*]

Reg. [*Embracing* ADRIENNE.] Then is our happiness complete. We shall never part again.

Dol. And I will, at last, leave my bachelorhood and worship at the shrine of my charming Anastasia!

Anas. [*Falls in his arms.*] You dear man!

Cor. [*Aside.*] She throws true nobility aside [*pointing to himself*] for such a presumptuous old fool! Oh! woman! woman! [*Sighs deeply and walks aside.*]

Hen. [*Leading* HILDA *forward. To* MORRIS.] If you will allow me, let me add my joy to the already o'er-flowing cup! Hilda has— [HILDA *pulls his coat.*] I beg your pardon—Alice has promised to administer to my future joy, with your permission!

Morris. [*Joins their hands.*] Bless you, my children!

Adri. [*To* REGINALD.] Dearest Reginald! The joy I have found in the new born love for my noble husband will make me never regret that it was by force of impulse that I was led to accept your heart and hand!

Reg. Let the agony of the past be buried in the joy of the present. [*To audience.*] And if you will forgive the impulse that led me from my post of duty, there will not be a cloud to obscure the sunshine of our future happiness.

Morrell. The end has justified the act.

Dol. I, too, have left my post of duty—but let the result be an extenuation of my desertion.

Morrell. [*Takes him by hand.*] Yes! I overlook it freely! and I feel satisfied that He, who watches over us all, will not censure us for being led BY FORCE OF IMPULSE!

Tableau.

	Morris.		Reg.	
	Col. M.		Adri.	
Henry.				Anas.
Hilda.				Doller.
Adol.				Corio.
R.		C.		L.

Curtain.

NEW PLAYS.
PRICE 15 CENTS EACH.

THE TRIPLE WEDDING.
A DRAMA, IN THREE ACTS, BY CHARLES BARNARD.

Four male, four female characters—Leading juvenile man, comic old man, first and second comedians; leading juvenile lady, two walking ladies and servant. Plain room scene; modern costumes.

The plot is novel and ingenious, the situations well worked out, and the interest continuous.

SYNOPSIS.—Act I., The Trust; Act II., The Search; Act III., The Wedding. Time of performance, one hour and a quarter.

SECOND SIGHT; OR, YOUR FORTUNE FOR A DOLLAR.
A FARCICAL COMEDY, IN ONE ACT, BY BERNARD HERBERT.

Four male and one female characters—Light comedian, low comedian, Irishman, Mexican nobleman and juvenile lady. Scene: A Clairvoyant's Parlor in New York. Time of playing, one hour.

The frantic efforts of Mr. Birdwhistle, a timorous music teacher, to escape the fury of Don Fiasco de Caramba, an untamed Mexican; the dismal predicaments of Dionysius O. Rourké and the clairvoyant scenes will keep the audience in a continuous ripple. Companies in search of a serious piece should NOT select this play.

WANTED: A CONFIDENTIAL CLERK.
A FARCE, IN ONE ACT, BY W. F. CHAPMAN.

Six male characters, viz.: Eccentric old man, with a partiality for proverbs; Irishman, "dude," shabby genteel comedian, talkative "sport," and clerk. No scenery required. Time of playing, thirty minutes.

A capital farce, containing none but "star" parts, with scope for easy character acting, racy dialogue, funny situations and comical "business."

A LESSON IN ELEGANCE.
A COMEDY IN ONE ACT, BY BERNARD HERBERT.

Four female characters—A butterfly of fashion, comic servant, old lady and unsophisticated young widow. The scene (interior, is laid at Newport in the height of the season.

Consists purely of light comedy, is bright and brisk in action, with plenty of "business," and has a *dénouement* as unexpected as it is welcome. The play can be effectively staged and costumed, if desired. Time of representation, thirty minutes.

BY FORCE OF IMPULSE.
A DRAMA, IN FIVE ACTS, BY H. V. VOGT.

Nine male and three female characters, viz.: Leading and second juvenile men, old man, genteel villain, walking gentleman, first and second light comedians, heavy character, low comedian, leading and second juvenile ladies and comic old maid.

A thoroughly good drama, worthy of the best talent. The action takes place during the period of the late civil war, the scene being laid partly in the army. Well adapted to the use of G. A. R. posts, though not confined to them in interest. The plot is interesting and well developed; the situations are striking; the "business" is effective, and every tableau will fetch an *encore*. Time of representation, two hours and a half.

Copies of any of the above Plays will be mailed, post-paid, to any address, on receipt of the price.

HAROLD ROORBACH, Publisher,
9 MURRAY STREET, NEW YORK.

Illustrated Tableaux
FOR AMATEURS.

A NEW series of *Tableaux Vivants*, by MARTHA C. WELD. In this series each description is accompanied with a full page illustration of the scene to be represented. The introduction of Part I. is the most complete and practical treatment of the subject ever written. The books are the best of the kind published, and should be in the hands of everybody about to arrange an entertainment of this kind.

NOW READY.

PART I.—MISCELLANEOUS TABLEAUX.—Contains General Introduction, 12 Tableaux and 14 Illustrations. Price, 25 Cents.

PART II.—MISCELLANEOUS TABLEAUX.—Contains Introduction, 12 Tableaux and 12 Illustrations. Price, 25 Cents.

A Few Opinions.

"Excellent Manuals."—*Book Chat.*

"Two Pretty Little Volumes."—*Cincinnati Inquirer.*

"Admirably suited for the purpose intended."—*Albany Argus.*

"Mrs. WELD is a well known adept in this kind of entertainment."—*New York Evangelist.*

"These small volumes form a complete assistant to any one desirous of giving tableaux."—*St. Louis Republican.*

"They will be helpful to young people preparing this pleasant method of entertainment."—*Christian Register.*

"Will be of much practical use and value to schools and persons interested in social amusements for church or home."—*N. Y. School Journal.*

"They will be of service for private entertainments. The directions as to dress and posing are full, and the illustrations will be very helpful."—*Hartford Courant.*

"They contain all the directions which can possibly be necessary to enable a company of amateurs to successfully present a number of tableaux of a varied character."—*Troy Times.*

"When we finished the second we wished we had a couple more. They are as indispensable to the amateur as a salary and a return ticket are to the professional."—*Puck.*

"As there is just now a revival of the olden time amusement of tableaux, these two little volumes come in just at the right time. Nothing pertaining to tableaux has been forgotten or left out. To persons interested in this kind of amusement, the little books will prove invaluable."—*New Orleans Picayune.*

"To any one who contemplates indulging in tableaux, these little books of Mrs. Weld's will be invaluable. So clearly does she explain the minutiæ, that a manager under her guidance may feel all the confidence which experience can bring. The writer is especially explicit in showing how the effects of scenery and costume may be secured with the simplest of material, so that the degree of expense may be made a matter of choice."—*Buffalo Express.*

MISCELLANEOUS GOODS.

☞ *An illustrated descriptive price list of miscellaneous articles, Wigs, Beards, etc., and Scenery, will be sent to any address on receipt of a stamp.* ☜

Lightning for Private Theatricals..	$0 25	Multiform Cream.................	$0 50
" Flash Box...............	50	" Powder...............	25
Colored Tableau Lights...........	25	Artist's Stomps	15
" " Fire, per lb......	1 75	Hares' Feet........................	50
" " " " by Exp.	1 50	Powder Puffs.......................	25
Magnesium Lights	25	Miniature Puffs....................	15
Carmine...........................	30	India Ink	10
Dutch Pink........................	25	Lining Brushes	5
Ruddy Rouge.....................	30	Cosmetique........................	25
Mongolian........................	30	Rouge de Theatre	25
Fuller's Earth.....................	30	Blanc de Perle.....................	25
Burnt Cork.........	40	Hair Powder.......................	50
Paste Powder.....................	30	Eyebrow Pencils...................	25
Nose Putty........................	25	Bleu pour Veins................	75
Lip Rouge, domestic..............	25	Fard Indien........................	75
" imported	40	Make-up Boxes.....$1.50, 4.00 and	5 00
Clown White......................	40	Grease Paints, 30 tints, 8 in. sticks:	
Dry Whiting......................	25	Flesh Colors.....................	35
Powdered Antimony..............	30	Lining Colors....................	20
" Blue....................	25	Grease Paints, set of 9 necessary	
Spirit Gum........................	30	colors....	1 00
Email Noir.......................	30	Scenery, Printed on Paper, per	
Joining Paste	25	set.......................$7 50 to 12 00	
Moustache Masks.................	15	Scenery, Painted on Canvas, per	
Water Cosmetique................	25	set...... ....$8 00 to 75 00	
Cocoa Butter.....................	25		

☞ *Canvas Scenery is delivered by Express only. Paper Scenes and the Make-up Boxes can be sent by mail at a slightly increased expense for postage.* ☜

THEATRICAL WIGS.

LADIES' WIGS.

Court...........................	$6 00	Short Curly........................	$5 50
Ringlet...........................	5 50	" with Parting...........	6 25
Frou-Frou........................	5 50	Plain Long Hair...................	7 50
Bourgeoise	7 50	Wig made up in Present Fashion .	5 00
Peasant Girl	7 50	Wench	5 00
Mother-in-Law....................	5 50	Frontals...........................	2 00
Witch	3 75		

GENTLEMEN'S WIGS.

Court Wig, with Bag or Tie	$4 00	
Rip Van Winkle	4 00	
Peasant	4 00	
Monk	4 00	
Judge	7 50	
Bald	4 00	
Comic Bald	4 00	
Chinaman	3 00	
Crop	4 00	
Dress	4 00	
Indian	$3 50	
Fright	5 00	
Irish	4 00	
Yankee	4 00	
Flow	5 00	
Scalp	2 00	
Negro	1 00	
" Extra Quality	1 50	
" White or Grey	1 50	
" with Top Knot	1 50	

BEARDS, WHISKERS & MOUSTACHES

Full Beard, without Moustache, on Wire	$1 75
" " " Ventilated	2 50
" with " on Wire	2 00
" " " Ventilated	2 75
Side Whiskers and Moustache on Wire	1 50
Short Side Whiskers on Wire	75
" " " Ventilated	1 00
Mutton Chop Whiskers, Ventilated	1 50
Chin Beard, Ventilated	1 00
Moustaches on Wire	35
" Ventilated	40
Imperials	25
Throat Whiskers	75

WIGS AND BEARDS TO RENT.

For terms and discounts see separate list, which will be mailed to any address on receipt of a stamp.

BY FORCE OF IMPULSE.

A Drama in Five Acts, by H. V. Vogt.

Price, 15 Cents.

Nine male, three female characters, viz.: Leading and Second Juvenile Men, Old Man, Genteel Villain, Walking Gentleman, First and Second Light Comedians, Heavy Character, Low Comedian, Leading and Second Juvenile Ladies and Comic Old Maid. Time of playing, Two hours and a half.

SYNOPSIS OF EVENTS.

Act I. Love vs. Impulse.—Dollerclutch's office.—A fruitless journey, a heap of accumulated business and a chapter of unparalleled impudence.—News from the front.—A poor girl's trouble and a lawyer's big heart.—Hilda's sad story.—"I'll see this thing through if it costs me a fortune!"—A sudden departure in search of a clue—The meeting of friends.—One of nature's noblemen.—Maitland betrays his secret by a slip of the tongue.—The ball at Beachwood.—Two spooneys, fresh from college, lose their heads and their hearts.—"Squashed, by Jupiter!"—Trusting innocence and polished villainy.—The interrupted tryst.—An honest man's avowal.—A picture of charming simplicity.—Murdell and Hilda meet face to face.—"I dare you to make another victim!"—A scoundrel's discomfiture.—Tableau.

Act II. The Separation.—The Maitland homestead.—Anastasia's doubts.—A warm welcome and its icy reception.—Forebodings and doubts.—Father and son.—Searching questions.—A domestic storm and a parent's command.—A foiled villain's wrath.—Enlisting for the war.—The collapse of the cowards.—"It's no use, 'Dolphy, the jig's up!"—Hilda's sympathy and Adrienne's silent despair.—The result of impulse.—The father pleads for his son.—Anastasia and Dollerclutch.—Coriolanus comes to grief.—Good and bad news.—Husband and wife.—Reginald demands an explanation.—A hand without a heart.—The separation.—A new recruit—Too late; the roll is signed.—Tableau.

Act III. Duty vs. Impulse.—Four years later.—A camp in the army.—Longings.—"Only six miles from home!"—The skeleton in the closet.—A father's yearning for his child.—A woman-hater in love.—Dollerclutch's dream.—A picture of camp life and fun.—Coriolanus has his revenge.—News from home.—Dollerclutch makes a big find. "Eureka!"—Proofs of Hilda's parentage and marriage.—A happy old lawyer.—"I'll take them to Hilda!"—Detailed for duty.—A soldier's temptation.—The sentinel deserts his post.—The snake in the grass.—"At last, I can humble his pride!"

Act IV. The Reconciliation and Sequel.—At Reginald's home.—News from the army.—"Grant is not the man to acknowledge defeat!"—Adrienne and Hilda.—False pride is broken.—The reconciliation.—"Will Reginald forgive me?"—Dollerclutch brings joy to Hildn's heart.—"You are the daughter of Morris Maitland!"—The stolen documents and the snake in the grass.—"Hang me if I don't see this thing through!"—A letter to the absent one.—Face to face.—The barrier of pride swept down.—"Reginald, I love you; come back!"—The happy reunion.—An ominous cloud.—"I have deserted my post; the penalty is death. I must return ere my absence is discovered!"—The wolf in the sheepfold.—A wily tempter foiled.—A villain's rage.—"Those words have sealed your doom!"—The murder and the escape.—Dollerclutch arrives too late.—The pursuit.

Act V. Divine Impulse.—In camp.—Maitland on duty.—The charge of desertion and the examination.—"I knew not what I did!"—The colonel's lenity.—Disgrace.—News of Adrienne's murder is brought to camp.—Circumstantial evidence fastens the murder upon Reginald.—The court-martial.—Convicted and sentenced to be shot.—Preparations for the execution.—'God knows I am innocent!"—Dollerclutch arrives in the nick of time.—"If you shoot that man you commit murder!"—The beginning of the end.—"Adrienne lives!"—A villain's terror.—Adrienne appears on the scene.—"There is the attempted assassin!"—Divine impulse.—The reward of innocence and the punishment of villainy.—Good news.—"Hurrah, the war is over; Lee has surrendered to Grant!"—The happy *denouement* and *finale*.—Tableau.

Copies mailed, post-paid, to any address on receipt of the advertised price.

HAROLD ROORBACH, Publisher,
9 MURRAY ST., NEW YORK.

THE ETHIOPIAN DRAMA.
PRICE 15 CENTS EACH.

1 Robert Make-Airs.
2 Box and Cox.
3 Mazeppa.
4 United States Mail.
5 The Coopers.
6 Old Dad's Cabin.
7 The Rival Lovers.
8 The Sham Doctor.
9 Jolly Millers.
10 Villikins and his Dinah.
11 The Quack Doctor.
12 The Mystic Spell.
13 The Black Statue.
14 Uncle Jeff.
15 The Mischievous Nigger.
16 The Black Shoemaker.
17 The Magic Penny.
18 The Wreck.
19 Oh, Hush; or, The Virginny Cupids.
20 The Portrait Painter.
21 The Hop of Fashion.
22 Bone Squash.
23 The Virginia Mummy.
24 Thieves at the Mill.
25 Comedy of Errors.
26 Les Miserables.
27 New Year's Calls.
28 Troublesome Servant.
29 Great Arrival.
30 Rooms to Let.
31 Black Crook Burlesque.
32 Ticket Taker.
33 Hypochondriac.
34 William Tell.
35 Rose Dale.
36 Feast.
37 Fenian Spy.
38 Jack's the Lad.
39 Othello.
40 Camille.
41 Nobody's Son.
42 Sports on a Lark.
43 Actor and Singer.
44 Shylock.
45 Quarrelsome Servants.
46 Haunted House.
47 No Cure, No Pay.
48 Fighting for the Union.
49 Hamlet the Dainty.
50 Corsican Twins.
51 Deaf—in a Horn.
52 Challenge Dance.
53 De Trouble begins at Nine.
54 Scenes at Gurney's.
55 16,000 Years Ago.
56 Stage-struck Darkey.
57 Black Mail.
58 Highest Price for Old Clothes.
59 Howls from the Owl Train.
60 Old Hunks.
61 The Three Black Smiths.
62 Turkeys in Season.
63 Juba.
64 A Night wid Brudder Bones.
65 Dixie.
66 King Cuffee.
67 Old Zip Coon.
68 Cooney in de Hollow.
69 Porgy Joe.
70 Gallus Jake.
71 De Coon Hunt.
72 Don Cato.
73 Sambo's Return.
74 Under de Kerosene.
75 Mysterious Stranger.
76 De Debbil and De Faustum.
77 De Old Gum Game.
78 Hunk's Wedding Day.
79 De Octoroon.
80 De Old Kentucky Home.
81 Lucinda's Wedding.
82 Mumbo Jum.
83 De Creole Ball.
8 Mishaps of Cæsar Crum.
85 Pete's Luck.
86 Pete and Ephraim.
87 Jube Hawkins.
88 De Darkey's Dream.
89 Chris. Johnson.
90 Scippio Africanus.
91 De Ghost ob Bone Squash.
92 De Darkey Tragedian.
93 Possum Fat.
94 Dat Same Ole Coon.
95 Popsey Dean.
96 De Rival Mokes.
97 Uncle Tom.
98 Desdemonum.
99 Up Head.
100 De Maid ob de Hunkpuncas.
101 De Trail ob Blood.
102 De Debbil and de Maiden.
103 De Cream ob Tenors.
104 Old Uncle Billy.
105 An Elephant on Ice.
106 A Manager in a Fix.
107 Bones at a Raffle.
108 Aunty Chloe.
109 Dancing Mad.
110 Julianna Johnson.
111 An Unhappy Pair.

THE AMATEUR AND VARIETY STAGE.
PRICE 15 CENTS EACH.

Afloat and Ashore.
Aladdin and the Wonderful Lamp.
All's Fair in Love and War.
Bad Temper, A
Babes in the Wood, The
Blue-Beard; or, Female Curiosity.
Caught in his own Toils.
Closing of the "Eagle."
Dark Deeds.
Eligible Situation, An
Fairy Freaks.
Fireside Diplomacy.
Frog Prince, The
Furnished Apartments.
Girls of the Period, The
Happy Dispatch, The
Harlequin Little Red Riding Hood.
Harvest Storm, The
His First Brief.
Ingomar (Burlesque).
Jack, the Giant-Killer.
Last Drop, The
Katherine and Petruchio (Burlesque).
Last Lilly, The
Little Red Riding Hood.
Little Silver Hair and the Three Bears.
Love (Burlesque).
Loves of Little Bo-Peep and Little Boy, The
Lyrical Lover, A
Marry in Haste and Repent at Leisure.
Matched, But Not Mated.
Maud's Command.
Medical Man, A
Mischievous Bob.
Monsieur Pierre.
Mothers and Fathers.
Out of the Depths.
Penelope Ann.
Pet Lamb, The
Poisoned Darkies, The
Result of a Nap, The
Robin Hood; or, The Merry Men of Sherwood Forest.
Slighted Treasures.
Three Temptations, The
Tragedy Transmogrified.
Two Gentlemen at Mivart's.
Virtue Victorious.
Wearing of the Green.
Wine Cup, The
Women's Rights.
Wrong Battle, The
VARIETY.
All in der Family.
Big Bananna, The
Decree of Divorce, The
Dot Mad Tog.
Dot Quied Lotchings.
Dot Matrimonial Advertisement.
Gay Old Man am I, A
Leedle Misdake A
Mad Astronomer, A
Lonely Pollywog of the Mill Pond, The
Mulcahy's Cat.
Ould Man's Coat Tails, The
Spelling Match, The

Any of the above will be sent by mail on receipt of the price, by

HAROLD ROORBACH, Publisher,
Successor to ROORBACH & COMPANY.

P. O. Box 3410.   9 Murray Street, New York.